BORN TO BE FREE

BORN TO BE FREE

Jack Miller

LEXINGTON BOOKS
Lanham • Boulder • New York • London

Published by Lexington Books
An imprint of The Rowman & Littlefield Publishing Group, Inc.
4501 Forbes Boulevard, Suite 200, Lanham, Maryland 20706
www.rowman.com

Unit A, Whitacre Mews, 26-34 Stannary Street, London SE11 4AB

British Library Cataloguing in Publication Information Available

Library of Congress Cataloging-in-Publication Data

Names: Miller, Jack, 1929– author.
Title: Born to be free / Jack Miller ; preface by James W. Ceasar ; epilogue by Michael L. Andrews.
Description: Lanham, Maryland : Lexington Books, 2018. | Includes bibliographical references and index.
Identifiers: LCCN 2018032154 (print) | LCCN 2018037580 (ebook) | ISBN 9781498575911 (electronic) | ISBN 9781498575904 (cloth : alk. paper) | ISBN 9781498575928 (pbk. : alk. paper)
Subjects: LCSH: United States—Politics and government. | United States—Politics and government—Study and teaching. | Political culture—United States.
Classification: LCC JK31 (ebook) | LCC JK31 .M48 2018 (print) | DDC 320.973—dc23
LC record available at https://lccn.loc.gov/2018032154

♾™ The paper used in this publication meets the minimum requirements of American National Standard for Information Sciences—Permanence of Paper for Printed Library Materials, ANSI/NISO Z39.48-1992.

Printed in the United States of America

CONTENTS

PREFACE

James Ceaser

What could lead someone already well into the age of retirement to create from scratch a new organization, put up millions of his own hard-earned dollars to fund it, and persuade many donors and foundations to join in—all to promote the teaching of America's founding political principles in higher education?

Until a decade ago, I would have had no answer. Then I met Jack Miller.

The occasion was a gathering of selected college professors who were invited to Chicago to assess the condition of civic education at our colleges and universities. No one doubted that this education was in dramatic decline. Fewer courses were being offered in the political history of the founding period and the philosophy of American government, requirements in these areas were being eliminated, and the number of new PhDs focusing on America's political origins was diminishing. The publication of serious research on the Founding in scholarly journals was also falling. The professors attending the summit all bemoaned this state of affairs, but few believed that the situation could be reversed. Graduate programs in history and political science had by now shifted their focus to different concerns, while the universities and colleges had developed other priorities.

One proposal made it through the day's deliberations. Why not bring together in a summer seminar the graduate students still interested in the American Founding and have them meet with some of the leading scholars in the field? Morale could be boosted as students realized that there were others who shared their interests, and there would be an opportunity for sustained discussion and real education. The seminar would add to what universities were not—or were barely—doing, enhancing the intellectual content of a small but dedicated remnant. The academics at this meeting imagined, of course, that if anything were ever to come of this idea, it would take a long period of planning and the fortuitous appearance of some very unlikely donors. On this somber note the summit concluded.

A couple weeks later I received a phone call from someone connected to Jack Miller. Jack, it turns out, had sponsored and attended the summit. He wanted to send a simple message. The seminar plan was a go—not for the distant future, but for the coming summer! Funding would be provided, and it would be up to a few of us professors, with some help from Jack's staff, to find the students, recruit the faculty, and prepare a plan of study. This was my first encounter with a real-life businessperson who possessed practical capacity and a sense of urgency. Something, I learned, could get done quickly, which was a different world from the large state university at which I worked, with its teams of administrators and multiple bureaucracies demanding endless consultations.

The academics at the Chicago meeting had a worthy though modest idea. Jack Miller had a much larger vision. Rather than give up on universities and colleges and retreat to an enclave, Jack's long-range plan was to work with and through them. The summer seminar was a step in beginning this process. Jack saw that, while institutions of higher education were no longer committed enthusiasts of civic education for their students, neither were most of them inveterate opponents. If someone could offer the incentives, demonstrate genuine student interest in the courses, and identify a motivated and interested faculty, an increasing number of universities and colleges might support the teaching of the American Founding, its background, and its influence. The indifference of deans could turn to acceptance and in some cases enthusiasm. We professors had allowed pessimism to set limits on our expectations. Jack Miller saw possibilities beyond what any of us could imagine.

Jack Miller's capstone work, *Born to Be Free*, offers his reflections on the American Founding, describes the formation and purpose of the Miller Center, and presents an autobiographical sketch of his life. This may sound like three books in one, but the different parts are held together by the common theme of freedom. Freedom is at the center of Jack's own beliefs, his freedom and the equal freedom of all Americans. How freedom can be secured and what people must do to keep it alive are the underlying themes of this book. Jack spends a good deal of time looking back at our history and his life, but the book's focus is on what is needed going forward. At eighty-nine years old, Jack is always looking at what will come next. The book speaks especially to "future leaders of the Miller Center, [and] future donors and others who have a passion for

America." Jack aims to set out "a clear guideline for what the Miller Center is and should always be."

The section of the book Jack devotes to the American Founding has a remarkable background story of its own. In a surprising admission, Jack reveals that though he attended a good high school and university, for some reason he never had a formal class on early American history or the philosophy of the Founding. His academic preparation at the University of Illinois at Champaign was spent almost exclusively in subjects related to business management, not the liberal arts. Jack counts this fact a great deficiency, though not one he realized at the time. In his mid-seventies, in tandem with beginning the Miller Center, Jack undertook an unusual personal project: educating himself in the intellectual origins of America's political foundations. The Miller Center's academic program became his university. Along with his wonderful wife Goldie, a highly successful businesswoman in her own right and an enthusiastic supporter of the Miller Center, Jack has attended a part of every Summer Institute that the Miller Center has sponsored, and in many summers there was more than one. Jack spent time talking to each of the students and meeting with the different faculty members. He read the assignments, and he went on to his own studies of Montesquieu, John Locke, and the works of many of the Founders and experts on the American tradition, from Jefferson to *The Federalist Papers* to Abraham Lincoln. This commitment to learning continues to this day.

There is as well an interesting sidebar to Jack's self-education project. The question naturally arises of what led him, *before* he began these studies, to form an organization devoted in the first instance to promoting the academic study of America's Founding. The whole project is unusual and improbable. Part of the answer may be that in Jack's youth, during and after World War II, patriotism was everywhere in America, whereas today, as he notes, the situation is obviously very different. It takes no knowledge of the theories of the Founders to believe that the current indifference to civic education could be part of the problem.

Jack realized that appreciation of country depends on instilling a culture, which must be taught "just as you would do in a business, in a family. . . . It is the culture that has made America stand out among nations and it is a culture worth reinforcing and preserving." But a stronger answer still is that Jack knew from his own life experiences that this country had given him something very dear, the opportunity to make his way up and achieve prosperity. He is filled with the feeling of wishing to give back, not from guilt but from gratitude. A similar impetus exists among many of those who have contributed to the Miller Center. There is a desire at bottom to return a moral debt and do what one can to sustain what is so precious.

Jack proceeds in *Born to Be Free* to consider the Declaration of Independence, the political philosophy of John Locke, and the American Constitution. The Declaration for him is the nation's great "mission statement." Like a business plan, it sets forth the country's basic aims and goals. At this document's core is the promotion of freedom, and it is no coincidence that the value Jack cherishes undergirds America's own creation. "To me, the most important concept guiding our Founders' actions . . . was that of the freedom of the individual." Much of the background to the Declaration, as Jack recounts, is informed by the political philosophy of John Locke. Jack has learned much from him, both in the areas of politics and political economy. Locke saw the worth of freedom, beginning with each person's ownership of himself, and Locke proposed a mode of government that sought to protect rights so far as possible, limiting some freedoms so that the greater part of them could be practically enjoyed.

At the same time, Jack has relied on his own experience to emphasize that a society will only be able to maintain its freedoms if most citizens approach things with a sense of responsibility. Responsibility is the brake on freedom that keeps it from swerving out of control. Jack begins his book on this note: "Responsibility is the key word. My parents could send me to school, but it was my responsibility to learn. I could get a job, but it was my responsibility to do a good job and earn more." Each person, in Jack's view, has his or her freedom and the need to accept responsibilities, except those who are unable to do so. Helping them, Jack says, becomes his responsibility.

As for the Constitution, Jack sees it as an ingenious document that aims to implement the goals of the Declaration. It provides government with sufficient power to perform its duties, while endeavoring to make sure that the power is watched and checked, so that no person or institution has too much of it. The separation of powers for Jack is one of the great bulwarks of freedom. So, too, is federalism, which divides power between the federal government and the states. Jack is a forceful advocate of the virtues of federalism, and while he acknowledges its great historical flaws in the history of slavery and civil rights, he laments how much power has otherwise been removed from the states and assumed by the national government.

Great as the Constitution is, Jack attributes part of the blame to some of its expansive clauses, such as the provision for providing for the general welfare, which have been used or abused to build an overbearing national state. Jack worries today about a national administrative apparatus that rules in many areas outside the scope of statutory law and without citizens' active consent. The threat is not only that we live increasingly today under this arrangement, but that so few Americans notice it.

In the second part of *Born to Be Free*, Jack describes the creation and functioning of the Miller Center. Its full name, I can now reveal, is "the Jack Miller Center for the Teaching of America's Founding Principles and History." Its heart or administrative base is a small, permanent staff of twelve persons that works out of the central office in Philadelphia. This apparatus, headed for many years by Retired Rear Admiral Mike Ratliff and now directed by Dr. Michael Andrews, is one of the great strengths of this operation and a key to its success. Many are the foundations that have fine goals and plans, but little capacity to execute them. Some suffer from being too small, others from being too large. The Miller Center staff has gotten it just right. The secret is an organization of highly competent and devoted workers that does not drain too much of the Center's resources. The staff carries out the ideas and plans of the Miller Center's Board, which include organizing conferences, finding and assigning the funding for postdoctoral fellows at major universities and colleges, interfacing with some of the nation's leading research libraries—the Newberry in Chicago, the Huntington in San Marino, the Rockefeller in Williamsburg, and the American Philosophical Society in Philadelphia—to promote research fellowships, and organizing and funding programs on campuses in recognition of Constitution Day.

The main activity of the staff, however, is tending to the maintenance and growth of the Miller Center "network." The network is the growing number of professors in America who are associated with the Center and are involved in teaching courses related to the American Founding, its philosophical background, and its effects. There are today some nine hundred professors on more than three hundred campuses who are involved. Many of them are former students from the Summer Institutes, and others have been faculty that the Miller Center has contacted. The essence of the program is identifying faculty members interested in the teaching of the Founding and suggesting to them how they can begin to grow this interest into a larger program of study on their campus. The Miller Center offers some assistance in getting going and it provides information and advice on program building, from expanding the curriculum to inviting speakers to encouraging undergraduate study and research.

Most of the "work" of the Miller Center, however, is performed by faculty members proceeding on their own initiative, raising funds, setting up local organizations, and above all teaching courses. In addition to all else it does, the central office acts as a mechanism that informs, supplies models for building local programs, and facilitates communication among professors who are now aware of a growing national movement. It is perhaps easy to understand how, even with just the small amount of assistance provided in many instances, the expansion of the Miller Center demands far more in funds than Jack can supply.

The Miller Center, as all should know, is no longer a family affair, but a public foundation that raises funds from hundreds of contributors and other foundations. This strength will ensure its future.

Two other activities of the Miller Center deserve mention. One of them is the recent attention the Center has begun to give to high school education. The same decline in civic education experienced at the college and university level has been evident in many of our high schools as well, and many of the persons that the Center contacts have expressed their concern at this development. The Miller Center's avenue of approach here, beginning in and around Chicago, is to use its network of college professors to begin programs of instruction on the American Founding for high school teachers. Many of the participants use these programs to acquire training in a subject they never received in college, while others find in them an opportunity to enhance and improve their skills with persons of the same rank.

The other function should prove of great interest to donors in higher education, many of whom wish to give substantial gifts to one institution, often where they attended undergraduate school. The difficulty they encounter is making sure that their intended contribution finally supports the purposes they wish to promote and is not, over time, diverted to some other program. For contributions in its general area of its interest, the Miller Center has shown that it can provide an invaluable service. It has negotiated on the donor's behalf with the designated institution to make sure that the plan for spending is worthwhile and meets the donor's wishes, and it then distributes the contribution on a schedule as the conditions are adhered to. Nothing in the long run does more to help donors and to maintain the integrity of the philanthropic process.

The final part of *Born to Be Free* is Jack's own personal story. Those who know Jack also know that he is a modest person who in no way wishes to call attention to or celebrate himself. Sensitive to this fact, he resisted including this section. But he was no doubt persuaded to proceed because this section illustrates something about America that is too often forgotten. "The story of my life is not exceptional nor do I consider myself exceptional in any way. Many in America have a similar story, made possible because America is the country it is." The country dimension shines through, but it fortunately does not diminish the great interest in following a person at a certain period of time, observing how he interacted with his parents and family in a section of Chicago, how he made his way through college, and how from modest means he began to find his way up economically in society. The account depicts a slice of American life, from travel and adventure, boyish pranks, a passion for exercise, hard work, marriage, children, temple, building a remarkable business, selling it, death of a spouse, remarriage, "retirement," and philanthropy. It is a story not to be missed.

Of the more abstract lessons that can be learned from Jack's account, one stands out for its sociological and theoretical importance. There is much discussion in this section about a commitment to hard work, a trait of Jack's, and what might be called business acumen, part of which is acquired by learning from mistakes. But Jack never says that hard work and business acumen are guarantors of success. Many who work hard and have business acumen never become multimillionaires.

As Jack's story shows, a number of accidents and fortuitous events happened to him along the way that put him in a place where success became possible, just as others no doubt encountered an opposite fate. There is no perfect relationship in this economic system—or any economic system—between merit and becoming wealthy. But it is still the case that once in a certain place, hard work and business acumen are needed to get ahead and that success rarely comes without them. Independence and hard work were requisites for Jack's achievement. "I present my story simply as being representative of what can be achieved in a free society based on a freemarket economy. Nothing more and nothing less." This is reason enough to extol economic freedom and to work for its preservation.

ACKNOWLEDGMENTS

This whole book is an acknowledgment of appreciation, an appreciation of the country where I was born and grew up, a country where individual freedom is the highest ideal, a country where we are continuously striving to make it possible for everyone to achieve their highest potential, if they are willing to invest the time, the effort, and their abilities to achieve it.

So, to start with, I would be remiss not to acknowledge my grandparents, who had the gumption to leave their homes in Russia (my paternal grandparents) and the Ukraine (my maternal grandparents) to come here, in the period around 1900. Without their initiative to do that, my story would not have happened.

And then there are my parents, Ben and Ida Miller, who gave me the freedom to grow and develop in my own way, who allowed me to find my own path—sometimes bemused, but always supportive. Plus, there is my brother, Harvey, who became my partner almost from the very beginning of Quill, and my brother, Arnold, who joined us later. Without them, the company would never have become as successful as it did, and I would never have had the resources to start and continue to support the Jack Miller Center, which this book is really all about.

And then there are all the people I have met along the journey of developing the JMC into the powerful influence it has become. There's the irrepressible Mike Ratliff, who, before his retirement in 2017, headed up the center from the very beginning in 2004. A retired Rear Admiral who was in charge of Naval Intelligence, Mike is an incredible person to work with. A suggestion to Mike becomes a much-improved reality in record time. No detail is too small nor opportunity too big for Mike. Not only was he key to the success of JMC, but also his suggestions for this book have made it a much-improved effort from what I originally submitted.

Then there is Mike Andrews, the new president of JMC, who has headed up the effort to train and help the hundreds of young postdocs—those who will teach our young people—and help them find positions on campuses across the country. He has been with JMC from the beginning. His intellect and commitment to liberal education have been invaluable. And the rest of the highly dedicated staff at JMC has played a crucial role in its success. In a sense, I am writing this book to thank them for their commitment to our mission of advancing the teaching of America's founding principles and history, and so that those who will come after them will understand that mission and how important it is for our nation's future.

Very important are all the highly intelligent, often brilliant, and always very dedicated, young, as well as seasoned, professors dedicating their lives to teaching upcoming generations about the extraordinary genius of what our Founders gave us and how we have struggled to make it a reality. I owe so much to them that it would be hard to repay it. They helped me understand what a great gift my grandparents gave me by immigrating here.

I have participated in discussions with, studied with, and exchanged ideas with so many that it would be impossible to mention all of them. But I would like to single out a few. First and foremost is Jim Ceaser, Harry F. Byrd Professor of Politics at the University of Virginia, who sits on our Board of Directors, teaches at our Summer Institutes, and has selflessly given his time to mentor the hundreds of young scholars who have participated in our work to expand the availability of a profound education in our history and principles. Jim has developed syllabi that have become the gold standard, which many professors around the country use for teaching our founding principles.

Professor Gordon Wood, the Alva O. Way University Professor Emeritus at Brown University, and recipient of the 1993 Pulitzer Prize for History, is the pre-eminent scholar alive today on American history. He has given unstintingly of his time, teaching at our Summer Institutes and lecturing around the country. Seven remarkable professors, whose work on behalf of our mission to advance the study and teaching of America's founding principles and history has been invaluable, also proofread the section on "What I Have Learned" and gave helpful suggestions and corrections. These include Ralph Lerner, Benjamin Franklin Professor Emeritus at the University of Chicago; Michael Zuckert, Nancy R. Dreux Professor of Political Science at Notre Dame University and editor of

American Political Thought: A Journal of Ideas, Institutions, and Culture; Richard Samuelson, Associate Professor of History at California State University, San Bernardino; and Bill McClay, Professor and G. T. and Libby Blankenship Chair in the History of Liberty at the University of Oklahoma and, like Jim Ceaser, a stalwart member of our Board; Scott Yenor, Professor of Political Science from Boise State University and Stuart Warner, philosophy professor and director, Montesquieu Forum, Roosevelt University. Their suggestions greatly improved this book. Any errors that remain are the responsibility of the author.

There are many donors who have helped JMC make the impact it is having; too many to mention them all. But I would be remiss not to mention just a few who have been outstanding: John Lillard, Tom Smith, Rich and Nancy Kinder, Tom Klingenstein, and Andrea Waitt Carlton, who have generously supported education to advance the teaching of America's founding principles and history. I want to thank my brother, Harvey, for his generous support, particularly on behalf of our Postdoctoral Fellowships and in getting the High School Teachers Initiative off the ground.

And then there is Dick Uihlein, whose transformative gifts have helped propel us along much-needed paths. Thank you, Dick.

I must also thank those who have served on our Board of Directors, helping to guide our work. Having the advice of two college presidents on the Board, John Agresto and the late John Strassburger, as well as the former chairman of the National Endowment for the Humanities, has been invaluable in shaping our successful approach to higher education. Similarly, having the support of remarkable businessmen and philanthropists such as John Lillard, former chairman of Wintrust, and Thomas Smith, founder of Prescott Investors, provided a unique philanthropic perspective.

A complete list of current and past directors follows below, but I want to especially thank Doug Regan, our vice-chairman, Michael Weiser, our Treasurer, and Jim Ceaser and John Agresto, members of our Governance and Nominations Committee, who are building and strengthening our Board of Directors to assure that the Jack Miller Center will be here for many years to come because we realize that, as Ronald Reagan said, "Freedom is never more than one generation away from extinction. We didn't pass it on to our children in the bloodstream. The only way they can inherit the freedom we have known is if we fight for it, protect it, defend it and then hand it to them with the well-taught lessons of how they in their lifetime must do the same" (Reagan 1961).

The job of the Jack Miller Center will never be done. It can just be improved upon, year after year.

ACKNOWLEDGMENTS

I would like to thank all the current and past board directors of the Jack Miller Center:

Michael Andrews
John Agresto
James Ceaser
Bruce Cole
Richard Fink
John Lillard
Goldie Wolfe Miller
Alicia Oberman
Doug Regan
Thomas Smith
John Strassburger (*in memoriam*)
Michael Weiser

In closing, my wife Goldie provided support and encouragement as I worked through the writing process and her vision and wit were always appreciated, thank you Goldie. And I also want to thank you, Goldie, for reminding me that the hard work and dedication of my assistant, Jennifer Olsen, should be acknowledged. Well done.

INTRODUCTION

Jack Miller

At eighty-nine years of age, as I look back on my life, it is apparent to me that I have lived it all as I saw fit, from the beginning to now, while shouldering the responsibilities for doing so. Sure, in the early years, before I was able to make decisions and do things for myself, my parents assumed those responsibilities. But, as quickly as possible, I seemed to have taken control.

Responsibility is the key word. My parents could send me to school, but it was my responsibility to learn. I could get a job, but it was my responsibility to do a good job and earn more. I could make money, but it was my responsibility to save so that, when I got married, I could afford a down payment on a home and then make the payments. We got married by a Rabbi, so I felt it was my responsibility to join a Temple, so that one would be there when I needed it.

I felt life was that way. I wanted the freedom to shape my own life and I accepted the responsibilities that went along with that. I also felt that others should have the same freedom and accept the same responsibilities. The only exceptions, I felt, were for those who had a real handicap that made it impossible for them to do so. Helping them was then my responsibility.

In my office, I have a statue, on a pedestal, of the torso of a man chiseling the rest of himself out of a block of bronze. I call it "The Self-Made Man." He is handsome and muscular—doing a great job so far, but he still has a way to go, and I suspect he will never finish. I look at it and actually touch it every time I am at the office. To me that represents my ideal in life.

And, so from telling a bit about my life—to our founding principles, to the Jack Miller Center for Teaching America's Founding Principles and History (JMC).

"All Men are created equal." Some are stronger while others are weaker, some more gifted than others in many ways, some born into better circumstances. But in this country they all were created to be equal before the law, whether man-made or divine.

"They are endowed by their Creator with Life, Liberty, and the Pursuit of Happiness." "Life." We each get it, a gift that no one should be able to take from us without just cause. "Liberty." No one is born as a slave to someone else. That was the vision, the mission and the dream. It took us many years to achieve this, but we finally did. And finally, "the Pursuit of Happiness," the ability to improve our position in life through our own efforts.

That vision, which I have since learned came down to us from the Hebrew Bible, the Greek philosophers, the English Magna Carta, the Enlightenment writers and more, was, without me knowing it, how I have lived my life. And like the statue in my office, the vision is an unfinished work, and it will not be finished in my lifetime. But as it says in *The Ethics of the Fathers* (*Pirkei Avot*), "It is not for you to complete the task, but neither are you free to stand aside from it" (Sacks 2015, 54), more wisdom from the past.

And so, I am writing this book to memorialize why I started the Miller Center and why I have invested so much money and time in it, so that future leaders of the Miller Center, future donors, and others who have a passion for America as it was conceived, have a clear guideline for what the Miller Center is and should always be, and also so that my grandchildren and theirs can grow up in a country as great as America has been, but is not guaranteed to remain.

This book, which has been called "three books in one," is divided into three parts. The first section is about what I have learned about our country's vision, our Constitution and our history, the struggle, the victories, and in some cases, the failures involved in trying to achieve that vision. All of it has truly been an amazing experience for me. The second part is about the Miller Center—how we started, our principles, our growth, and our vision for the future. And the third part is the story of my life and what led me to start the Miller Center. It may be a bit long, but, I hope, not tedious. The story of my life is not exceptional, nor do I consider myself exceptional in any way. Many in America have a similar story, made possible because America is the country it is.

Now more than at any time in the span of my life, as America and Western civilization in general are under attack from some of those without and from too many within (who "know not what they do," to give them some slack), we need to remind ourselves and teach our young people what the promise of America is.

America was built on a certain culture of self-reliance, hard work, the rule of law, and the belief that "all Men are created equal" and have an opportunity to improve their position in life through their own effort. And as in any culture, in order to continue, it must constantly be taught and reinforced, just as you would do in a business, in a family, everywhere. It is the culture that has made America stand out among nations, and it is a culture worth reinforcing and preserving.

WHAT I HAVE
LEARNED ABOUT
AMERICA'S FOUNDING
PRINCIPLES
AND HISTORY

In the fourteen years since the beginning of the Jack Miller Center, it has been my privilege to meet one hundred or so full professors and about eight hundred young postdocs and new professors, almost all of them in political science and American history. It is through attending twenty-five Summer Institutes, reading the material, and enjoying the many lunch and dinner conversations with the other participants, that I have come to learn and appreciate what a wonderful form of government our Founders gave us.

In this section I discuss just a portion of what I have learned over these past fourteen years. But it is, I feel, at the core of what has made America such a unique and great country. Our Founders didn't invent these principles; they just synthesized thousands of years of thought and experience, starting with the five books of Moses, into a great national experiment. And it has worked for over 240 years. Our challenge is to preserve it and to develop its promise.

1

THE DECLARATION OF INDEPENDENCE AS OUR MISSION STATEMENT

I was fortunate, very fortunate, to be born in a country that was itself born with a mission and a vision of the freedom of each individual embedded, as the reason for its being, in the document declaring its independence from its mother country. In the second paragraph of our Declaration of Independence are the thirty-six words that would forever change how a free people would think of themselves:

> We hold these Truths to be self-evident, that all Men are created equal, that they are endowed by their Creator with certain unalienable Rights, that among these are Life, Liberty, and the Pursuit of Happiness.

Of course, I had read those words at some point in grade school and may have read them in high school (but I don't remember if I did), and I never read them in college. But nowhere was I taught what they really meant. It was only after I started the Jack Miller Center for Teaching America's Founding Principles and History, as a result of a spur-of-the-moment decision (more about this later), that I really began to understand their meaning.

It was an expensive decision, costing me over thirty million dollars, already invested and pledged, with more to come, even after my death. And this has been more than matched by other donors as we work to enrich the education of our young people on the principles that have made this country so great. For me personally, it has been a great educational experience, teaching me how my experience of living free to pursue my own destiny was made possible.

My "classroom" has been the twenty-five Miller Center Summer Institutes my wife Goldie and I have attended over these past fourteen years, studying, discussing, and mingling with some of the finest professors in the country who focus on America's founding principles and history. Plus, we have been meeting and participating in discussions with almost five hundred young professors, many of whom are now on the path to tenure or are already tenured professors in their field, which has been thoroughly enlightening and enjoyable. And then, of course, there is the massive amount of reading of original documents required of all attendees of these Summer Institutes—and my newly inspired desire to read and learn all I could about our Founding and our history.

All of that has more than made up for what I didn't learn in school about the principles on which this country was founded, the principles that have made it so great, the principles that have more recently been so trampled upon and which we are in danger of losing. These are principles that seem to have been part of my DNA right from the beginning, principles that I have lived my life by. I did so without realizing they were the principles that some of the greatest philosophers in history, as well as our Founders, believed were the basis of a free society. So let me, in my unscholarly way, give you my understanding of those principles.

It took me a long time to understand what our Founders gave us, but it finally sank in. They gave us a Declaration of Independence, which was written first and foremost as our mission statement. In only 1,458 words they laid out America's mission, declaring all individuals equal before the law and free to live their lives as they saw fit, so long as they allowed others to do the same. They then gave us a Constitution, a set of guidelines so we could, through self-governance, realize that mission. And finally, they gave us a Bill of Rights to protect us against an overzealous government.

To me, as I kept reading about it and discussing it with professors and postdocs, it was, above all, about the individual. It was not about groups. It was about the rights of the individual who, in order to secure the vast majority of those rights, willingly gave up a few, to form a society, a government. It was about getting that balance between what rights we give up and those we retain as individuals, rights that are so critical and which we fight over so often.

The overarching, simple structure our Founders gave us, as I understand it, is of a government based on the concept of personal freedom best expressed in those thirty-six words in the second paragraph of our Declaration of Independence: "We hold these Truths to be self-evident, that all Men are created equal, that they are endowed by their Creator with certain unalienable Rights, that among these are Life, Liberty, and the Pursuit of Happiness."

It doesn't say all groups of people. It says, "all Men," meaning all individuals. Then the first paragraph, or preamble, of our Constitution states, "WE, THE PEOPLE of the United States, in Order to form a more perfect Union, establish Justice, insure domestic Tranquility, provide for the common defense, promote the general Welfare, and secure the Blessings of Liberty to ourselves and our Posterity, do ordain and establish this Constitution for the United States of America."

In other words, they established the Constitution, the first *written* constitution in the world, and the first government formed by the consent of the governed. That Constitution laid out the outline for what kind of government was needed in order to realize those ideals in the Declaration.

"WE, THE PEOPLE" means that "we," as individuals, want to form a "more perfect Union"—meaning that the Articles of Confederation were inadequate. So, we as individuals are willing to give up certain rights to achieve the important goals listed. But, as the Bill of Rights made plain, we weren't willing to give the government free rein to tell us what to do in most areas of our lives.

It is that second paragraph of the Declaration and the first paragraph of the Constitution that have made me increasingly and passionately love and respect what our Founders gave us. They also are why I have come to believe that I must do all I can to oppose those who want to change their meaning through their own interpretations. Those two paragraphs set up the whole mission and the plan for our great country. That mission and plan have been under attack almost from the beginning. Alexander Hamilton, for example, understood that, while the Tenth Amendment limited the powers of the federal government, the commerce clause could be used to expand those powers. Also, he understood that another few words in the same Section 8 also formed a loophole that could be used to expand the powers of the central government in ways not anticipated by the Founders.

Those few words in Article I, Section 8, laid out the reasons Congress could tax the public: "The Congress shall have Power To lay and collect Taxes, Duties, Imposts, and Excises, to pay the Debts and provide for the common Defence and general Welfare of the United States." While the Founders were trying to correct a major weakness in the Articles of Confederation, which was the inability to raise money to pay for the costs of the Revolutionary War, they made a major blunder, in the opinion of many, by adding two words, "general Welfare," that were left undefined, and that opened the doors wide for almost unlimited taxation for any expenditure that the winds of the day made popular. The commerce clause and the general welfare wording have been the source for the almost unlimited expansion of the federal government over the years.

So—for me, to try to keep "a more perfect Union" going forward—my focus is on the education of our young people, so they can learn about and appreciate what our Founders intended.

The second paragraph of the Declaration goes on to say, "That to secure these Rights, Governments are instituted among Men, deriving their just powers from the consent of the governed." And, eleven years later, in 1787, they gave us a constitution that, along with the state governments, was designed to secure those rights. That Constitution was intended not only to give the central government enough power and the proper structure to perform its most basic responsibility of protecting citizens from foreign powers and domestic violence (i.e., within the United States), but also to restrain the federal government from usurping the power that belongs to the states and from stripping away the basic rights of citizens.

Thus, the Constitution limited the powers of the government to those enumerated in the legislative powers granted in Article I, and it provided some basic protections to citizens, for example, by protecting the writ of habeas corpus from arbitrary suspension. Then, with the addition of the Bill of Rights in 1791, additional restrictions on the power of the federal government were put in place in order to further protect the citizens from governmental abuse and high-handedness.

After all, according to the Declaration of Independence, the primary function of a government is to protect the individual from foreign and domestic threats by protecting the person and property of its citizens. The Founders were influenced by England's Magna Carta, signed by King John in 1215. The Magna Carta still forms an important symbol of liberty today and is held in great respect by the British and American legal communities. In 1956, Lord Denning (quoted in Lee 2015) described it as "the greatest constitutional document of all times—the foundation of the freedom of the individual against the arbitrary authority of the despot." We were building on the English achievement of establishing a constitutional monarchy and then going beyond it.

All of this I learned from reading the lessons and participating in the programs at the Summer Institutes. The concepts really are easy to understand. But simple concepts can become complicated when they are reinterpreted to suit the ideologies of the interpreters. Almost all of the Summer Institute seminars, speeches, and discussions were focused on reading and discussing the sources our Founders read and what they wrote, the original texts, not what some other writers interpreted them as meaning.

Many of our Founders were brilliant and extraordinarily well-read men, drawing their ideas from the accumulated wisdom of the ages, starting from the Hebrew Bible (the Old Testament) and the Ancient Greeks, the Magna Carta and the writings of the Enlightenment period, and more. The American Founders had the advantage of starting from a nearly clean slate and not being limited to amending a form of governance, such as the monarchy and the established church that had long existed in the motherland. They could build on the self-governing culture that had already grown up in this distant and somewhat isolated land, as Alexis de Tocqueville (whose work we studied at many of the Summer Institutes) so brilliantly explained in his description of American townships and the importance of localism in American political life. Building on English philosophy and American experience, the Founders certainly did not intend to form a government that other countries *should* follow, but that, in Washington's words, they *could* follow if they chose to do so.

We were also fortunate, as I learned at the Summer Institutes and from my own readings, that we were forming this government just as the Enlightenment was reaching its climax. I had never learned about the Enlightenment in school, but through the Miller Center I discovered that in the seventeenth and eighteenth centuries in Britain and elsewhere in Europe, thinkers such as John Locke, and later Adam Smith, were exploring the theme of liberty in both the state and the economy. In a beautiful coincidence, Smith, the Scottish philosopher and economist, published his famous book, *The Wealth of Nations*, in 1776, the same year that our Declaration of Independence was issued.

Benjamin Franklin was in London as the colonial agent for Pennsylvania from 1755 to 1765, roughly the years that Smith was in Glasgow and London, working on his book. Franklin knew many of the leading English and Scottish intellectuals, including Smith and David Hume. They and Franklin shared much in their general outlook on politics. They favored liberty for the individual and they also believed strongly in the free market. Not only Franklin, but most of our Founders were well versed in Locke and Smith and other Enlightenment thinkers, as well as in the Bible and the English common law.

From everything I learned from these readings and discussions at the Summer Institutes, I came to appreciate how extraordinary our Founders were. Most of them studied subjects in primary schools that people today don't even study in college, such as languages and great literature. In fact, what they learn in college now is often slanted because of all the speech code restrictions in place today, as well as the restrictions and protests regarding which politically correct speakers are allowed to lecture on campus.

Back then, and even during my days on campus, the only restrictions seemed to be that you should observe the normal, civilly acceptable forms of speech. Today it seems as if blasphemous and foul speech is okay but the free expression of contradictory ideas is not. What a strange turn of events for one of the places where the discussion and debate of ideas is supposed to take place so young people can learn and choose. I truthfully don't understand the extraordinarily weak response by the school administrators to the shutting down of free speech on campus, something that is so basic to our rights, and so basic to the purpose of the universities themselves.

At the time of the Enlightenment, as for many centuries before, people were ruled by a combination of the monarchy and the church. From the beginning of time, people had fears about this mortal life, and needed some reassurance and meaning for their lives. They first believed in various gods and idols, in which the people vested powers, so that these gods and idols could supposedly give them protection from nature and from other human groups, and so they might help them make sense of life, death, suffering, life after death, and so on. Then, as it's told in Genesis, monotheism was born when God appeared to Abram (Abraham). First, Judaism, and then Christianity, and later Islam came into being as monotheistic religions.

From that time until the late eighteenth century, societies almost everywhere were ruled by kings, nobles, and priests; everyone else was subservient. Faith, not reason, was the guiding force: faith in the King, faith in the Church. For our purposes, the most important characteristic of that period was that, almost universally, people died in the station in life into which they had been born. The royalty was the royalty and the peasant was the peasant, and that was that. The inability of the peasant class to earn and amass property is what kept them peasants. Our stated right in the Declaration to "the Pursuit of Happiness," Jefferson's way of more poetically saying, "the right to property," changed that for Americans.

The Enlightenment thinkers had a different idea about the old forms of society. To start with, they placed reason above faith. In his *First Treatise on Government*, Section 58, Locke wrote, "Reason . . . is [our] only Star and compass" (Locke 1988, 182) and as he stated further in the *Second Treatise on Government*, Section 6, it is a compass that can guide us in our moral and political lives:

> The State of Nature has a Law of Nature to govern it, which obliges every one: And *Reason, which is that Law*, teaches all Mankind, who will but consult it, that being all equal and independent, no one ought to harm another in his Life, Health, Liberty, or Possessions . . . [and] when his own Preservation comes not

in competition, ought he, as much as he can, to preserve the rest of Mankind, and may not unless it be to do Justice on an Offender, take away, or impair the life, or what tends to the Preservation of the Life, the Liberty, Health, Limb or Goods of another. (Locke 1988, 271; emphasis added)

"When his own Preservation comes not in competition," I would argue, means that man's first order of business is to take care of himself and his own needs without denying others the same rights. Or as Locke put it, "ought he, as much as he can, to preserve the rest of Mankind, and may not impair . . . the Life, or what tends to the Preservation of the Life, the Liberty, Health, Limb or Goods of another."

And from there, Locke proceeded to lay out what would provide the basis for Jefferson's "all Men are created equal" statement in the Declaration. In his *Second Treatise*, Section 4, Locke stated, "To understand Political Power right, and derive it from its Original, we must consider what State all Men are naturally in, and that is, a State of perfect Freedom to order their Actions, and dispose of their Possessions, and Persons as they think fit, within the bounds of the Law of Nature, without asking leave, or depending upon the Will of any other Man" (Locke 1988, 269). This is certainly an argument against serfdom or slavery.

He follows that up immediately in *Second Treatise*, Section 4, with another statement that it is "a State also of Equality, wherein all the Power and Jurisdiction is reciprocal, no one having more than another" (Locke 1988, 269). Men are free and men are equal, but they are also bound by a law of nature obliging them not to harm another. These three excerpts form the basis of his thinking, and the basis of our Declaration of Independence written just about one hundred years later, and of the fundamental truths of our politics.

There had been hints of Locke's three propositions in the thought of times past. Recall that when Moses came down from the mountain, he gave the law to all the people, not just to a select few priests. This would indicate that he thought all people were equal. Equality also found its way into Christianity, as in the Golden Rule. But taken altogether, Locke's three propositions added up to a novel and radical doctrine in his time.

Locke's radical thinking prepared the way for the shattering of many centuries of political practice. What a radical idea that all men are, by nature, created equal and that they, through their own actions, might change their position in life. In the *Second Treatise*, Section 27, Locke expressed that idea this way: "Every Man has a 'Property' in his own 'Person.' This no Body has any Right to but himself. The 'Labour' of his Body, and the 'Work' of his Hands, we may say, are properly his." And he goes on to say, "For this 'Labour' being the unquestionable Property of the Labourer, no Man but he can have a right to what that is once joyned to, at least where there is enough, and as good left in common for others" (Locke 1988, 28–88; quotation marks added).

The phrase, "where there is enough . . . left in common for others," seems to be purposely misinterpreted in recent discussions in the United States and elsewhere about income inequality. Many people complain about some individuals becoming very wealthy while others are left in poverty. Their complaint seems to be based on the belief that there is a limited amount of wealth in the world and if someone has more, then, necessarily, someone else must have less. But I, and most others who are not socialists, believe that there is always "enough . . . left in common for others," no matter how much any one individual has accumulated, at least in a free society such as ours.

The idea that "there is limited wealth so if someone has more, someone else necessarily has less" is a totally false concept. Wealth is infinitely expandable as people discover new sources of it. The computer revolution is a perfect example. Did Bill Gates take his wealth from someone else's pocket? Who is poorer because of the iPad or iPhone? I would suggest that many other people are richer because of them, even though Steve Jobs became extraordinarily rich. We do not live in a world of zero-sum wealth.

Locke argues that a person has a right to the property that he labors on and owns. When he goes on to say that "all Mankind . . . being all equal and independent, no one ought to harm another in his Life, Health, Liberty, or Possessions," it was but a short step from there to Jefferson's poetic phrasing in the Declaration.

Reading John Locke for the Summer Institutes turned out to be a fantastic treat. In fact, I could understand his writings more easily than I could understand those of some of the professors who try to interpret him. For anyone trying to understand our government, I highly recommend that they read John Locke's *Second Treatise*. It really is the basis for much of what is in our Declaration and our Constitution.

In short, our Founders were saying that all "Men" were able to improve their position in life through their own efforts and through the right to their property as the fruit of the labor of their self-owned bodies and minds. Jefferson, in substituting "Pursuit of Happiness" for "Property," did not mean to deny the Lockean claim to a natural right to property, for he himself on many occasions speaks of such a right.

So, there we have it, from what I have learned over these past fourteen years: the source and thinking behind those thirty-six words in our Declaration of Independence. Those words became the mission statement, the North Star, for our country to navigate by: "created equal," "Life," "Liberty," and "the Pursuit of Happiness." What did our Founders understand these words to mean and how have they been misinterpreted so much?

Locke helps us understand those words. His help is important because the Declaration is so brief in outlining a vision for a free society that many readers today are changing the meaning to suit their own idea of what our vision should be, thus blurring and even, at times, reversing our Founders' original intentions. My fear is that, if they succeed, then we will be following the wrong star, navigating toward a wrong, and far worse destination.

For Locke, "created equal" was that state "wherein all the Power and Jurisdiction is reciprocal, no one having more than another." No one by nature has more authority or rightful power than anyone else. (Seems as if Ayn Rand must have read Locke.) When government exists, that is no longer true—some are authorized to exercise power over others, but the embodiment of natural equality in civil society, as Locke called it, is equality before the law. Some may have more authority, but all are equally subject to the law. This concept can be traced back also to the Torah, the Hebrew Bible.

It is obvious that many other interpretations of the idea of "natural equality" make little sense. "Men" are unequal in many ways: some will be taller, others shorter. Some will have a beautiful singing voice while others, like me, can't carry a tune. Some can jump higher or run faster. Some are smarter than others. Given all the differences in the make-up of people, in their temperaments, in their abilities and in the circumstances into which they were born and raised, it was obvious to our Founders that outcomes in life would be different and unequal, yet all could be equally subject to the same law.

As some of the Miller Center professors put it, "There was no natural hierarchy, no natural claim of superiority of one man over another." Or, "They were equal to pursue that form of life that would please them, so long as they were socially responsible." "They had the capacity to improve their position in the world." "They had a fair start in the race, but weren't guaranteed a gold medal." Today, in our society, there are some who are clamoring for exactly the opposite, even starting in grade school, where, after a race or other event, everyone receives a trophy and where they have sometimes done away with having a valedictorian because that would draw attention to the fact that someone was smarter or worked harder.

2

LIFE WITHOUT LIBERTY LOSES ITS MEANING

Our Founders Protected Both

"They are endowed by their Creator with. . . . Life." The Sixth Commandment, in the Torah's version of the Ten Commandments, is "Thou shalt not murder." In other words, one's life is precious, and one of government's most important duties is to protect it. This is basic to the mission statement laid out in our Declaration and it came from one of the oldest texts known to man.

And what of Liberty? The word can be open to varying interpretations. For some, Liberty could mean getting, or staying, out of jail. For some, it could mean the liberty or freedom to do whatever they want—or licentiousness, the lack of legal or moral restraints.

In reviewing my notes from various JMC Summer Institutes, from my reading, and from watching some JMC video presentations featuring prominent scholars on the subject of Liberty, a fairly clear and consistent message comes through.

Liberty, as expressed in the Declaration, starts with Locke's concept that everyone owns himself. In other words, it is the opposite of slavery. No one is naturally subservient to anyone else. Or, as Jefferson said, "The mass of mankind has not been born with saddles on their backs, nor a favored few booted and spurred, ready to ride them legitimately, by the grace of [G]od" (Jefferson 1826).

As one professor put it, "All men are free to live their lives not at the command of others, but as best they can live them out themselves." Understanding liberty that way means not only do they have that liberty, but they also have a responsibility: if they want that liberty, they are responsible for what kind of a life they live, for what they achieve in life.

We are each responsible for our own life. "Our actions have consequences and we each are responsible for our own actions," as I always tell my children and grandchildren. They are probably tired of hearing this by now. Just as parents who give their children too much may tend to spoil them, so, too, does a government that makes people dependent on its social programs deprive them not so much of their liberty as of their ability to exercise their liberty well. Another lesson from the Founders is one that Tocqueville reinforced in his *Democracy in America*, when he warns against the new mild, but debilitating, despotism that modern democracy can produce (Volume 2, Part 4, Chapter 4): "The first, and in a way the only, necessary condition for arriving at centralizing public power in a democratic society is to love equality or to make it believed [that one does]" (Tocqueville 2000, 650).

And that takes us to the next, and last, phrase in our country's mission statement, which is the Pursuit of Happiness. This phrase points to a concept with a wide meaning—the right to pursue a way of life of one's own choosing so long as it does not impinge on the rights of others or on the genuine needs of society. It incorporates the right to Property, without which, our Founders felt, it would not be possible to improve one's position in life and therefore to achieve happiness. John Locke, who appears to have been the source of Jefferson's concept, wrote in the *Second Treatise*, Section 87, that people possessed natural rights to preserve "Life, Liberty and Estate" (Locke 1988, 323). "Estate," at that time, meant property in external goods of the world, which serve as the means of one's support, and thus as a necessary means to happiness.

In any event, the idea wasn't new with Jefferson. A few months before Jefferson wrote our Declaration, George Mason had included in the Virginia Declaration of Rights, Article I, the proclamation "that all men are by nature equally free and independent, and have certain inherent rights, of which, when they enter into a state of society, they cannot, by any compact, deprive or divest *their posterity* [emphasis is mine]; namely, the enjoyment of life and liberty, with the means of acquiring and possessing property, and pursuing and obtaining happiness and safety." Nothing could be clearer than this.

But whatever the source, it all comes down to the fact that you can't have liberty, or happiness, if you are controlled by others. And the only way you can gain that independence is by having the ability to support yourself through your own labor or through the income from property (wealth) you possess and certainly not by being dependent on government handouts. So, to me, the pursuit of happiness means the ability to improve my position in life, which comes from freedom and independence, which, for me, comes from acquiring greater income and property and the independence that this makes possible.

Of all the misery and unhappiness that I personally have witnessed, almost all of it comes from sickness or from arguments over money or the lack of it. Money is a wonderful, if not guaranteed, lubricant to grease the wheels of a friction-filled life. It is the means by which you can do much good, not only for yourself and your family, but for others as well. Once free to choose, people find happiness in various ways. I happen to love business and the process of building something, so that is where I find much of my happiness. I am still doing it now, with our real estate business, Millbrook, and with the Jack Miller Center.

In any event, the Declaration of Independence, which, as I have said, is the mission statement for our country, the North Star by which we should direct all of our actions, is very clear. It reflects centuries of thinking by many of the world's best moral philosophers. However, much lesser minds may try to change its meaning today by corrupting the meaning of the original words. A deep reading of all the sources, such as we encourage at the Miller Center, makes the meaning very plain. Our Founders understood it well.

3

THE CONSTITUTION

A Game Plan for
Realizing the Mission

The challenge the founding generation faced was to create a form of government able to realize that mission. They had just fought a war to free themselves from a monarchical government and knew that such a government was not what they wanted because it did not fit with the natural equality they had affirmed in the Declaration. They needed a strategic plan, to use business terms, to achieve that mission.

Their first effort at forming a government was crafted in the Articles of Confederation, drafted in 1776 and adopted by all the states by 1781. Within a few years it became obvious that the federal government was too weak to govern effectively since it had no power to raise any revenue at all via taxation. All it could do was to request funds from the states which sometimes complied, but often did not.

Each of the thirteen states considered itself to be free and independent. Under the Articles, they had formed a confederation, a loose union like an alliance, in order to fight the war for independence and then to (loosely) govern the nation. But these Articles proved unequal to the task.

For example, because the government couldn't impose taxes and because the states wouldn't live up to their obligations, there wasn't enough money to feed, clothe, and pay our troops during the Revolutionary War, much less pay for the materials of war. Our troops went hungry, often even shoeless. It was hard to negotiate loans from foreign countries and then even harder to pay them back. It was also almost impossible to make treaties with foreign governments since each state still considered itself to be independent and often failed to respect the terms of the treaties negotiated at the federal level. There were many other faults in the Articles, but these were the biggest.

So, in 1786, five states called for a convention to discuss ways to improve the Articles of Confederation. James Madison arrived in Philadelphia with a plan for a much greater overhaul, amounting to a new constitution. He knew that if he were to succeed in that endeavor, there must be a powerful person to head the convention, and the person needed was the hero of the Revolution, George Washington. Madison and others lobbied hard to persuade him to attend.

But Washington was reluctant even to attend, much less to be the president, until he became convinced that the convention was going to work toward significant change. As General of the Army during the Revolution, he had been totally frustrated by the weakness of the Articles. After a lot of backroom politics, Washington agreed to attend, and he was promptly and unanimously elected president of the convention.

The states had sent delegates to the convention with instructions to revise the Articles of Confederation. But when the delegates met, they immediately began to discuss a new constitution. To make the discussions open and frank, they agreed to a closed-door convention. No one was to take notes and they were not to discuss the proceedings with anyone outside of the convention delegates. So, for almost four months, from May 25 to September 17, 1787, they met in what is now known as Constitution Hall in Philadelphia, through the heat of summer, to come up with a new constitution, which has survived now for 241 years, making it the oldest written constitution in the world.

It's amazing that they could produce this revolutionary document in such a short amount of time. I can't even imagine how they could do it. But from the lectures of Professor Zuckert, who taught at the Summer Institute, and from some of the readings, it became clear to me that they didn't arrive empty-handed. James Madison was especially important to the reform effort. Before the convention he had ordered a crate-load of books on history, political philosophy, and more from his friend Jefferson, who was then in France. The knowledge he gained from reading these books prepared him to attend the convention with more insights than any of the other attendees on governing and forms of government, and why governments are formed in the first place. One of the blessings of not having TV in those days, I imagine, was that you had a lot of time to read.

Madison's study of previous examples of confederacies throughout history revealed to him that most failed because the authorities acted upon the member states as totally independent entities separate from the whole, just as the Articles did. The failure of the Articles of Confederation was not unique but followed a regular historical pattern. So he devised a new kind of federalism, which was, as he later described it, without example in world history. That served as the basis for the plan the Virginia delegates introduced early in the convention.

The solution that Madison devised was to have the federal government have a direct relationship with the individual citizens rather than just with the state governments. So the individuals who made up the citizenry of the states were also to be the ultimate source of power at the federal level. Again, the concept in our country is that it is not groups or states but the individual who is the basis of our government.

Thus, he invented the new kind of federalism that the American Constitution introduced to the world. Because of his new plan Madison has been acknowledged as the "Father of the Constitution." Moreover, he took very comprehensive notes on the proceedings in Philadelphia, something delegates were not supposed to do, so we owe him our gratitude for our knowledge of what happened. He was also the one who argued most strongly for many of the ideas in the Constitution.

4

OVERCOMING CHALLENGES THROUGH THE DISAPPEARING ART OF COMPROMISE

The Constitution is very short, with just seven Articles and a series of Amendments that are now twenty-seven in number. It is shorter than many legal contracts I have signed and also much easier to read. No "whereases" and "whereofs." But it wasn't easy to create this document because the delegates faced many significant challenges, and three in particular.

The first major challenge was to preserve the identity and powers of the states. The delegates were split between those who wanted a strong central government, the Federalists, and those who didn't, later called the Anti-Federalists. The Anti-Federalists were strongly states' rights people. In fact, once they realized that a constitution creating a stronger federal government was a foregone conclusion, several refused to sign it because it lacked a Bill of Rights. They agreed to sign only when they were assured that such a bill would be added soon after signing.

To them, I believe, we owe a great deal of gratitude for whatever restraint remains on our federal government from becoming too dictatorial and for protecting our individual rights.

In any event, four years after the Constitution was approved—again, under the leadership of Madison, but at the insistence of the Anti-Federalists—the Bill of Rights, that is, the first Ten Amendments, was added to the Constitution. The Bill of Rights guarantees certain individual rights to be inviolable by the federal government. The First Amendment, for example, protects freedom of speech and the right of "the people peaceably (a word often ignored today with impunity) to assemble." The Fifth Amendment guarantees due process of law, and together the Fifth, Sixth, and Seventh Amendments guarantee the right of trial by jury in both criminal and civil cases. The Tenth Amendment guarantees states' rights, the right of the states to all the powers not given to the federal government. If only they could have foreseen how some provisions in the Constitution, as well as court judgments, would be used over time to override this Amendment, they would have made it even stronger!

The second major challenge for the delegates was the question of slavery. If the Constitution was to carry out our mission statement in the Declaration, then slavery shouldn't exist in the country. But it did, and it was practiced by some of the greatest of our Founders: Washington, Madison, and Jefferson.

In the North, where slavery was less important economically, a nascent anti-slavery movement was beginning. By the early years of the nineteenth century, all the Northern states had plans in place to abolish slavery. But, given the convention's main purpose of establishing a union of all the states, the question of abolishing slavery in the entire nation would have been a total deal breaker and could not be on the table at Philadelphia.

The plain fact of the matter, also, was that any effort to immediately abolish slavery in this Constitution would lead to the dissolution of the convention and doom the union. The Southern slave-holding states would simply walk out. But, in order to have a union, and also express their disapproval of slavery they tried to finesse the situation—for example, by never once mentioning the word slavery in the Constitution.

The absence is obvious also in Article I, Section 9: "The Migration or Importation *of such Persons* as any of the States now existing shall think proper to admit, shall not be prohibited by the Congress prior to the Year one thousand eight hundred and eight, but a tax or duty may be imposed on such Importation, not exceeding ten dollars for each *Person*" (emphasis added). Notice the very roundabout way in which slaves were described. In plain English, Congress was given the power to prevent the importation of new slaves starting in 1808.

The Southern states had bought themselves another twenty years, by which time some of them hoped to grow much larger than the North, so they could then prevent Congress from exercising its power to ban the slave trade. In fact, however, Congress and President Jefferson acted to ban the slave trade on January 1, 1808, the very first moment the Constitution would allow it.

The third major challenge was the question of representation. The small states were afraid that the big states would overwhelm them in the voting process, and the big states felt that the voting should be based on population. After much conflict, this was resolved by creating two branches of the legislature. The Senate would include two individuals from every state regardless of population, while the number of delegates in the House of Representatives would be based on each state's population.

There was also a question of how to count the slaves in apportioning seats in the House. In a total switch of positions, the North, which for other purposes felt the slaves were equal, didn't want them to be counted as equals for the purpose of counting population, thus resulting in more representation in the House for the slave-owning South. And the South, which hadn't thought slaves equal, wanted them to be counted as equals.

A compromise was reached whereby each slave would be counted as three-fifths of a person. While the issue of slavery was too big a challenge at the time of the convention, the failure to address this issue proved to be the breeding ground for decades of animosity between North and South, and ultimately led to a calamitous Civil War that resulted in the deaths of seven hundred thousand Americans. The issue of slavery has come back to haunt us many times over.

5

THE CONSTITUTION
Protecting Us against Tyranny

> *"The accumulation of all powers, legislative, executive, and judiciary, in the same hands, whether of one, a few, or many, and whether hereditary, self-appointed, or elective, may justly be pronounced the very definition of tyranny."*
>
> —James Madison, *Federalist 47*

So, in just a few months, from May to September 1787, our Founders gave us a constitution, a constitution that has helped us remain relatively free these past 241 years. They faced some significant challenges, overcame them, and gave us a very good, concise document, a document that can easily conform to a small, breast pocket-sized booklet, a document rooted in the concept expressed in our Declaration of Independence about the freedom of the individual.

The best way to understand the Constitution and what our Founders were thinking is to read the *Federalist Papers*. These were a series of essays originally written as newspaper opinion pieces after the Constitution was drafted, but before it was ratified by the states. The intent was to convince the people, primarily in New York, that they should approve the Constitution. Written between October 1787 and August of 1788, mostly by Hamilton—with many contributions by Madison and a few by John Jay—they were published in newspapers in New York City, and then collected and published as a book. They are so important because they clearly and forcefully lay out the arguments in favor of the Constitution. They truly represent our Founders' thinking.

For example, they understood well that men were imperfect. They knew that power corrupts and that men who gained power would always want more power. They knew they had to guard against this. As Madison said in *Federalist* 51, "But what is government itself but the greatest of all reflections on human nature? If men were angels, no government would be necessary. If angels were to govern men, neither external nor internal controls on government would be necessary" (Rossiter 2003, 319). Over these past fourteen years, as I studied and talked with professors and young scholars, and read many of our founding documents and the writings that our Founders had read, writings by John Locke, Montesquieu, Adam Smith, and others, I gradually began to understand what our Founders were trying to do, and what kind of government they were trying to form. I also began focusing on what kind of government they envisioned and what kind of government we have evolved into, how far we have drifted away from their vision as well as how much we have, in some instances, realized it.

And during that time, I found myself drifting further and further away from the dinner-table conversations among my friends. Those conversations revolved around the issues of the day, abortion, chronic poverty, inner-city crime, education, etc.—all important issues. But my mind kept focusing on how too much power was flowing into too few hands, and how we, as individuals, were losing too many of our freedoms. This was exactly the opposite of what our Founders intended, and it is what they feared most. But when I mention this at these dinner-table conversations, everyone gets a vacant look in their eyes, listens politely, and then, when I am through, goes back to the usual topics. People today almost automatically look to the federal government to solve all problems, while I am more and more a proponent of states' rights, of getting the government closer to the people.

Our Founders understood people and human nature, and tried to form a government to protect the people against human shortcomings. In fact, our Founders distrusted power, distrusted government, distrusted majorities, and distrusted human nature. So, their challenge, as they saw it, was to protect people against these shortcomings in human nature. To do this, they created a form of government in which there were opposite and rival interests that could act as a check and balance on one another. As Madison wrote in *Federalist* 51, they wanted "ambition . . . to counteract ambition" (Rossiter 2003, 319). They built a government structured to limit the concentration of too much power in any one area.

Our Founders feared this concentration of powers so much that they went to great lengths to try to prevent it. The genius of what they created, American federalism, really hit the sweet spot between too much consolidation and too little. It divides the power of government in a number of ways and guards against too much power being concentrated in too few hands, while still allowing for the advantages of operating in combination.

To achieve this, they built three protections against it into our Constitution. The first was federalism, the separation of power between the federal government and the states, with a specific list of what the federal government was responsible for, with everything else left to the states or to the people. That was in the Tenth Amendment in our Bill of Rights.

Then there was the separation of powers between the legislative, the executive, and the judicial branches of government, purposely making each branch as independent of the others as possible. In Article II of the Constitution, for example, the president is elected by the Electoral College, which is, in turn, elected by the people directly. Congress has no say in that selection, so the president is completely independent of Congress and the Judiciary.

Finally, because they feared that the legislative branch would be the most powerful and would accumulate too much power over time, they split it into two separate branches, the Senate and the House. Each branch would have different election cycles, different terms of office, and different responsibilities (Article I). This also helped balance the power between large and small states by having two senators from each state, regardless of population.

Those protections were supposed to guard against "the accumulation of all powers, legislative, executive, and judiciary, in the same hands" (Rossiter 2003, 298), which they felt would lead to tyranny. James Madison, in *Federalist* 47, lays all of this out very plainly and completely. But over the years, through many administrations, the integrity of federalism and the separation of powers has been eroded. Also, unfortunately, too many of our "laws" are passed not by Congress but by bureaucrats in agencies set up by the president or Congress. These "laws" (rules) bypass the protections set up by our Founders.

This is what has become, in my opinion, one of the biggest dangers facing us today. Congress or the president sets up agencies to do certain jobs and then gives them the power to accomplish their goals. Then, people within these agencies devise rules and regulations that have the power of law. It's Congress that is supposed to pass laws, not some bureaucrat in some agency. So, we, the people, are subject to a spiderweb of laws so numerous, so vast, that none of us could possibly know all of them, and I would bet that not a single person in the country could get through a single day without breaking dozens of such laws— that is, unless we were passed out stone-dead drunk all day, and even then there are probably some rules or regulations we would be breaking.

So, insofar as the concept of federalism our Founders imagined is concerned, there has been, almost from the beginning, a steady erosion of it. For example, with more and more power flowing to the federal government and away from the states and the people, states' rights have been steadily attacked. In a very few instances, this has achieved some good, as for example, ending slavery and Jim Crow. But, for the most part, we would have been better off leaving the power at the state and local levels, where the people have more control.

This erosion has been engineered using the concepts in the Constitution, as I have mentioned before, for the general good, and the regulating of interstate commerce. This has opened the gates to a grab for power by the federal government. Then the fuel that has driven this engine has been money. The Constitution gave the federal government the power to tax for, among other things, the general good.

Wow, that means that the federal government could identify almost anything as being for the general good, and justify a tax for it. Once it has the money, it is in control. Education is a good example. Education used to be a local responsibility. However, since 1979, when President Jimmy Carter established it, we've had a Department of Education with the stated purpose that it "establishes federal policy for, administers and coordinates most federal assistance to education. It assists the president in executing *his* education policies for the nation and in implementing laws enacted by Congress" (U.S. Department of Education 2010; emphasis mine).

In practice, that federal assistance means that the federal government controls education, not the states and the local communities. And here the old saying, "He who pays the piper calls the tune," comes into play. More and more, the federal government is "calling the tune"—another blow to federalism as originally intended by the Founders.

This, of course, is in contradiction to what Madison thought would happen when he argued in *Federalist* 45 that "the powers delegated by the proposed Constitution to the federal government are few and defined. Those which are to remain in the State governments are numerous and indefinite" (Rossiter 2003, 289). He also predicted that the "operations" of the federal government "will be most extensive and important in times of war and danger; those of the State governments in times of peace and security" (Rossiter 2003, 289). This, of course, is not what has happened. In wartime and in peacetime, the federal government dominates. And this is a serious challenge to the concept of the freedom of the individual. Federalism and the separation of powers are not the most efficient form of government. A dictatorship is much more efficient. Federalism and the separation of powers mean that government is messier. It takes longer to get things done. There is a lot of discussion, compromising, and delay. But, in the end, hopefully we come up with greater protection for the freedom of the individual.

Also, with more governing responsibility handled at the state and local levels, more people in the country get involved in governing at various levels, and the whole nation becomes a testing area for finding the best practices. People sitting on local government bodies learn how self-government works.

With this idea of federalism and the separation of powers our Founders found a good blend, as I have said, the sweet spot between too much power in the central government and too little. So, federalism and the separation of powers are two great protections our Founders built into our Constitution, protections we should fight to preserve. But, I am afraid, too many of us don't know about these protections and don't appreciate the importance of them. Let's start discussing that kind of topic at some of our dinner parties.

To me, the most important concept guiding our Founders' actions, as I keep saying, was that of the freedom of the individual. Everything that they gave us in our Declaration and our Constitution was designed to protect that God- or nature-driven freedom. And while they recognized the need for government to better protect those rights—a government for which we were willing to give up a few of our rights in order to protect the vast majority—in their haste to write the Constitution they left the door open for tyranny to find its way in and take away many of those rights that were supposedly protected.

Our Founders recognized the problem they were facing. They were experienced legislators, and they were, as I have said, very well read. They knew, as Madison said so eloquently, "men weren't angels." They knew that power was corrupting and that you couldn't entrust people with too much power because they would always want more. And they knew that the accumulation of power in fewer and fewer hands would come at the cost of individual freedom.

So, that first barrier to the protection of our freedom, federalism—the separation of powers, state and federal—has been breached. Then the second barrier, the separation of powers between the branches of government, has also been under attack, with more and more power flowing to the president. This is especially true since the beginning of the twentieth century. More recently, the issuance of executive orders by the president has usurped Congress's responsibility to pass legislation. And, finally, there has been an increase in the expansion and reach of the many federal agencies in government today and all the rules and regulations they promulgate as *de facto* laws that the rest of us have to obey. (Think the EPA and IRS, for example.)

But to go back to what I have learned while participating in the Summer Institutes and lectures, this is how my studies have led me to my concern about what is happening. The Constitution was drafted, as I have said, with the view in mind that men were imperfect and that they would always pursue their own self-interest, not the greater good.

So, in order to protect against this very human trait of the pursuit of self-interest, and the lust for power, our Founders structured our government on the basis of separation of powers and checks and balances. This was one of the most important concepts in our Constitution to assure that we would be protected against the threats of a too-powerful government, protected against a tyranny. Again, as quoted above, Madison said in *Federalist* 47, "the accumulation of all powers, legislative, executive, and judiciary, in the same hands, whether of one, a few, or many, and whether hereditary, self-appointed, or elective, may justly be pronounced the very definition of tyranny." The concept of the separation of powers traces its origins all the way back to Biblical and classical times, when the Jews, the Greeks, the Romans—and then the English with the Magna Carta—all developed governments with the separation of powers. So, our Founders, who were extremely well-read men, had much to draw upon. Our Founders looked to the separation of powers as a great protection of individual freedom.

6

THE POWER TO
TAX AND THE
CONCENTRATION
OF POWER COULD
DESTROY FREEDOM

I have already mentioned a few areas where we have gone astray from the protections our Founders gave us. Still another is in the powers of taxation. Whereas, under the Articles of Confederation, the federal government had few taxing powers, under the new Constitution the taxing powers of the federal government were strong. Article I, Section 8, of the Constitution states, "The Congress shall have Power To lay and collect Taxes, Duties, Imposts and Excises, to pay the Debts and provide for the common Defence and general Welfare of the United States."

When it comes to understanding our Founders' reasoning regarding this provision, consider this theoretical argument: "Yes, of course, in a limited government there should be strong limits on taxes to prevent taxation being used to take property." And there is discussion of schemes such as the deliberate inflation of the currency as also being pure theft.

But the thinking also was that no cap should be put on taxation because: "You can never tell in advance how much money might be needed under some circumstances, say, for national security in time of total war; and therefore, you should not define, in the Constitution, an explicit limit on the amount that can be taxed. You have to rely here on the government, not the Constitution, to protect rights."

So, our Founders provided in our Constitution for procedures on how to levy taxes but not for any absolute limits. Our Founders were strong proponents of individual property rights and certainly never envisioned any form of socialism. But they had just fought a war that created a huge debt with a form of government created under the Articles of Confederation, which gave the government no taxing powers.

The only purpose of this unlimited power of taxation in the new Constitution was to allow Congress to collect as much in taxes as necessary to pay for the unknown cost of wars we might become engaged in. After all, our Founders had just gone through an agonizing period, during which the federal government did not have the power to collect taxes to pay for the costs of the Revolutionary War. In the new Constitution they tried to correct this, but it seems they overshot the mark.

As happens in many documents, there was some wording that opened the floodgates to unintended consequences. By including the phrase general Welfare along with the intended common Defense, they created an opportunity for almost unlimited taxing powers for all types of purposes they couldn't even have imagined or intended. Alexander Hamilton, a proponent of a very strong central government, recognized this immediately and knew it would suit his purposes.

This was a strange oversight, perhaps, for a nation that had fought for its independence over perceived misuse of the taxing power by the British government. Our Founders went to war because of what was seen as an unacceptable way the tax was imposed on tea, among other things. In any event, over the years the federal government has used this power of taxation to accumulate more and more power for itself and to try to reshape the country in the image they endorse at the moment.

As one example, which we have already mentioned, we can look to what has happened to education in this country. At first and for a very long while, education was the responsibility of the states, local communities, and the people. Today, the federal government takes money from citizens in local communities and then gives some of it back to the same local communities for educational purposes, but *with strings attached*, giving the federal government great influence over what is taught and how it is taught. This pressure for conformity on what is being taught to our young people is a dangerous threat to freedom in our country. Diversity of thought and civil discussion is the path to the greatest freedom. In Hitler's Germany and Stalin's Russia, we have powerful examples of the dangers of conformity in education and thought.

Hillsdale College in Michigan and Grove City College in Pennsylvania are two institutions that have consistently refused to take federal money and have remained free to teach what and how they want. They both endorse Judeo-Christian Western values and free-market traditions. Now, more colleges, particularly sectarian colleges, are refusing federal money so that the federal government won't be able to dictate what and how they teach. It is terribly dangerous for the government to control what our young people learn. That is what a totalitarian state does. Personally, I would be happy to see the Department of Education shut down and the power returned to the states and the communities, where the citizens have much more control over what is taught, therefore resulting in much more diversity of thought in our country, a very healthy condition.

This one example of aggrandized federal power is replicated many times over in almost every facet of our lives, with the result that the Tenth Amendment has been savagely neutered. Only lately have we seen some of the states fighting to regain some of their legitimate powers, as the states' attorneys general have begun suing the federal government for overstepping its legitimate powers.

But the problem isn't just the breakdown of federalism, the separation of power between the federal government and the state governments. Within the federal government there has also been an almost total breakdown of that separation of powers. Just as more and more power flowed up from the states to the federal government, so more and more power began to flow from the legislative branch to the executive branch.

The executive branch, which originally was charged with just executing and enforcing the laws, has today also begun to make the laws through executive orders and regulatory rules. This results in the creation, by unelected bureaucrats, of rules and regulations that have the power of law. Arguably, this has done more to hog-tie the free market than anything Congress has done.

In addition, the executive branch decides which laws, passed by Congress, it wants to execute and enforce. Perhaps our Founders wanted it that way, fearing that, of the three branches of government, it would be the legislative branch that would gain the most power. They were mistaken. Today, the president is in a position to almost single-handedly dictate much of the law of the land.

Then there is the Supreme Court, which was supposed to be the least political of the branches of government. It is supposed to provide protection against executive encroachment on legislative power and to be the protector of the individual's rights, as laid out in our founding documents, by ruling on the constitutionality of laws and other governmental actions. However, when we see court rulings consistently split between liberal and conservative justices, with the same justices always splitting into their respective camps, it doesn't take a genius to see that the court has become part of the political system rather than being an independent arbiter with defined guidelines in our Constitution and precedents.

Here is an example of how this works. I had the opportunity to have dinner, on two separate Miller Center occasions, with two justices of the Supreme Court who hold opposing views of their responsibilities as justices. I asked each of them what criteria they used in making their decisions.

One of them, Justice Scalia, said that he looks at what was written in the Constitution and what the words meant according to the intention of the Founders. The other justice said that he used several criteria. One criterion was what the Constitution said. Another was the judicial interpretations over time. But the criterion that he said he gave the most weight to, and the one that truly shocked me, was how the ruling would affect society. He was substituting his own judgment for that of the Founders, some of the best minds that the world has ever known, as well as for the text of the Constitution itself. What *chutzpah*, what gall, and what arrogance! But then, some people always feel that they are seeing things from a much higher moral plane than the common folk.

If justices who have been assigned the duty of deciding whether the laws are constitutional can make interpretations based on their own prejudices and policy views, then we are afforded little or no protection by having a written constitution. Hamilton said in *Federalist* 78 that the judiciary would be the "least dangerous" branch (Rossiter 2003, 464). Instead, it has joined with the other branches to further the concentration of power in federal hands and from there into the president's hands.

The courts have approved or looked the other way as presidents make laws through executive orders and decide whether or not to enforce those laws that are on the books. How like a monarchy. Another breakdown in the protection of the separation of powers!

7

IN SUMMARY

So these are just a few of the things I have learned over the past fourteen years as I attended the Miller Center's past twenty-five Summer Institutes, reading the material provided for the Institutes, plus a lot of other books and articles, and talking to some of the leading professors in the field and also to well-read, eager young postdocs and professors.

I must emphasize that my comments include not only what I learned about the beliefs of our Founders and their sources, but also my interpretations of their thinking. The beauty of what we do at the Miller Center in terms of teaching is that we work only from original texts, not from what other scholars interpret those texts to mean. We want students to read *The Federalist Papers*, *The Anti-Federalist Papers*, the Constitution, the Declaration of Independence, and the writings of Washington, Jefferson, Madison, and other Founders. We want them to go back and read what our Founders were reading, the sources from which they drew inspiration. They should read Locke, Adam Smith, Montesquieu, and other Enlightenment thinkers. They should go back to the Torah (the Old Testament). Then they should draw their own conclusions.

This is a part of what every—yes, every—program of higher education here in the United States should include as a required course. It should also be taught in our high schools. It's what every citizen needs to learn in order to be a good citizen. It is what we need if we are to preserve the freedoms our Founders intended us to have.

There are many other trends in the country that also worry me a good bit. One trend that especially worries me is the growth of the politically correct speech codes that are now used to shut down free expression on many campuses across the country. In many cases, that is in direct contradiction to our First Amendment rights that there should be "no law respecting an establishment of religion, or prohibiting the free exercise thereof; or abridging the freedom of speech." Another protection that is being thrown under the bus. For the life of me, I can't understand how we are raising children who are so delicate that they can't hear an opposing opinion without having a nervous breakdown. And I don't understand how those who are supposedly in charge of our schools put up with this, since the exchange of ideas and reasoned discussion are supposed to be the basis of learning.

Also, I am a believer in the importance of culture to any endeavor. Even before we were a separate nation, Americans were forming a culture favoring independent, responsible people. Benjamin Franklin remains a model and proponent of what we were as a people, freedom-loving and self-reliant. That culture came not only from the ideas of Western civilization as formed from the Magna Carta and English law and from the Enlightenment and the Bible. It arose also because we were separated from most other countries by big oceans. We had learned to be self-sufficient. We had learned to rule ourselves, because there was no one around but us.

This culture of independence and self-reliance helped propel us towards becoming a great nation. The new immigrants who came to this country from many different nations yearned for this same freedom. While most didn't find the streets paved with gold, they at least found the hope that they or their children could enjoy the Pursuit of Happiness, the opportunity to improve their position in life through their own efforts.

During my own early years, we proudly called ourselves the melting pot of the world. When people came here speaking many different languages, we didn't become a tower of Babel but, instead, everyone learned English—poorly at first, perhaps, but very well by the second generation. Everyone wanted to become a part of the American culture. Maybe, in my early days, we called ourselves Italian-Americans or Polish-Americans or Irish-Americans or Jewish-Americans, but most importantly we were Americans. There was an American culture we all embraced. We studied it in our schools. We studied our history, both the good and the bad. We studied our Declaration and our Constitution, perhaps not fully understanding them, but appreciating the fact that we were free.

These days we don't study our history and our Declaration and our Constitution in many of our schools. In fact, you can be a history major in many of our universities without ever studying American history, much less civics.

Today we hear a lot about Americans being a multicultural society. I beg to differ. We are a multiethnic society and should have just one culture, the

American culture. If we go down the road of being a multicultural society, we will become a fractured nation that will break up into warring subsegments. Only people who want to be a part of the American culture should come here to become citizens or should be allowed to remain here.

Even Emma Lazarus in her sonnet, "The New Colossus," which is inscribed on the Statue of Liberty, didn't think we should allow just anyone to enter the United States. She wrote, "Give me your tired, your poor, / Your huddled masses yearning to breathe free" (Lazarus 1883). "Yearning to breathe free"!— not those seeking to change our culture of freedom, not those seeking to do us harm. Our doors are open only to those who want to "breathe free," who "yearn to be free," who want to be part of our culture and add to it. Yes, those people, but not others, we welcome. I could go on with many other examples of the fractures appearing in the foundations of our country. But those few are enough.

I believe that our Founders put in place the best form of government ever devised to support the individual freedoms that are so much desired by most people. The reason individuals form governments in the first place is to protect those freedoms. The Founders formed this government to protect the "natural rights" so clearly defined in our Declaration of Independence.

In summary, it is critical to remember and to teach each new generation that our Founders gave us a Constitution that was bookended on one side by the Declaration of Independence and on the other side by the Bill of Rights. To understand the government they gave us, you must first start with the vision for our country contained in the words of the second paragraph of our Declaration, "that all Men are created equal" and that they have "certain unalienable Rights." This is the whole purpose for forming a government at all.

Then there is a Constitution, which is written down, for, in the words of that same paragraph of the Declaration, "to secure these Rights, Governments are instituted among Men, deriving their just powers from the consent of the governed." The key concept here is that it is the people, "the governed," who have and retain all the power. The Declaration goes on to say, "That whenever any Form of Government becomes destructive of these ends, it is the Right of the People to alter or to abolish it, and to institute new Government," to achieve their "Safety and Happiness." Our Founders gave us such a document in our Constitution.

But then, just to make sure that people's rights were explicitly protected, they added the Bill of Rights, the first Ten Amendments to the Constitution. As I have said, this was insisted upon by the Anti-Federalists who, rightly, as it turns out, feared a central government that would be too powerful.

So those three separate documents, read together, give us the mission statement for our country, the rules of government that would help us achieve that mission, and the added protection for the individuals who make up the citizens of our great country. Read together, along with some of the political philosophers and thinkers our Founders read, they give us a strong understanding of what has made our country so wonderful.

I believe strongly that unless our young people are taught what those freedoms are and learn how our government was designed to protect them as our Founders intended, then those freedoms will be lost.

The older generations are already set in their beliefs and are tugging the nation in one direction or another. It would be difficult, but not impossible, to change their views, although we might encourage some to fight harder for freedom. But the younger generation, if exposed to the ideas of freedom on which our country was founded, could find its way back to that path.

And now, at the age of eighty-nine, looking back over a lifetime of independence and hard work that has led me to what I consider some success in life, I see that path being destroyed. It truly saddens me that our mission statement, the North Star that was supposed to guide us in our journey through life, has been so badly mangled and distorted by so many, and because of the way it is misinterpreted today by so many, it is leading us in a false, destructive direction.

In the process of writing this book, I have had to reread and rethink much of what I have learned over these past fourteen years, and it has made me more fully realize why I believe as I do. Our country was formed primarily on Lockean views that favored a complete break from the prevailing monarchical/church hierarchy. But Locke's views, in my opinion, didn't come from pure reason with no basis in past history. Locke and many of his contemporaries were versed in Hebrew and read the Torah and other Hebrew writings, such as the Talmud. They read Greek and Roman history. They read the Magna Carta. And then they used their minds and reason to synthesize what they learned and develop all of that into a coherent political philosophy. Our Founders, then, were the beneficiaries of all of that historical evolution.

So I believe that people who want radical change from what our Founders established are ill-informed and are endangering our country. Our Founders understood that they were developing an imperfect document that would be carefully interpreted over the years. They provided for amending the Constitution, but purposely made it difficult so there would be a lot of consideration and discussion before amendments were made. Our country has grown strong and vibrant because of our way of life, our American culture. I believe that we should continue to protect what our Founders have given us, that wonderful freedom of the individual to pursue his or her happiness as he or she sees it, without interfering with another's right to do the same.

Of course, that is how I interpret what I have read and what I have gleaned from the many discussions over these past fourteen years. Others may interpret things differently. And, as I have already mentioned, that is what is so great about the Miller Center approach. We ask people to read the original documents our Founders read. Study what thinkers and historians throughout the millennia have to say, what history and human experience has to teach us. Read what our Founders themselves had to say—and *The Federalist Papers* are a good place to start. That is the Miller Center approach. Original documents! Not others' interpretations of them.

Personally, I believe that our Founders gave us a form of government that is best suited for allowing people to reach their fullest potential if they so desire. It allows them the greatest freedom to live their lives as they choose, in pursuit of what Aristotle calls the ultimate goal, happiness. But this form of government is constantly being challenged by those who think they have a better way. And that is fine, but first one should truly understand what one already has and what one stands to lose before making a choice.

It is for that reason that I am investing in the Miller Center a good portion of what would otherwise be my grandchildren's inheritance or a grander lifestyle for Goldie and me, to get the teaching of our founding principles and history back into our educational system. My hope is that they and their children and their children's children can enjoy the kind of life I have had in a country as wonderful as the one I grew up in.

Maybe, if we work hard enough to educate our young people about the real meaning of those thirty-six words in our Declaration, it will be possible for our young people to know what they truly mean so that we don't go off course and lose our freedom.

And that is why I started the Miller Center and have devoted so much time and money to its success. I hope and pray that it will be my legacy to this country, whose founding principles I love so much.

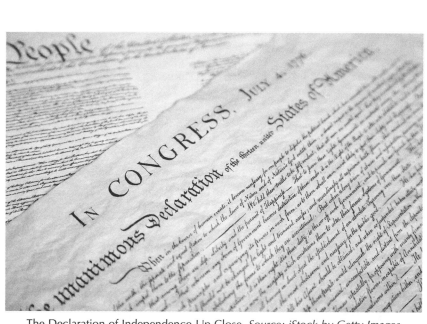

The Declaration of Independence Up Close. *Source: iStock by Getty Images*

Signing of the Declaration of Independence. *Source: iStock by Getty Images*

Founders Discussion. *Source: iStock by Getty Images*

Washington Crossing the Delaware. *Source: iStock by Getty Images*

Portrait of Abraham Lincoln. *Source: iStock by Getty Images*

THE JACK MILLER CENTER

My Legacy to the Country

"Building the engine that will enrich what our young people learn about our founding principles and history, the concepts that underlie and support a free people, the concepts that have made our country so great."

—Jack Miller

In this section I talk about the Jack Miller Center for Teaching America's Founding Principles and History. We started the center fourteen years ago in 2004, despite the fact that most of the nearly fifty professors we had called together to discuss the plan said that the chances of success were slim to none, in anticipation of strong opposition to the teaching of American founding principles and history.

But we have proven those predictions wrong. Sure, on a few campuses we have met with resistance. But at the vast majority of colleges and universities we have been welcomed. There are many reasons for this, but first and foremost, we've succeeded because our goal is to enrich their programs. (Few are even offering courses in America's founding principles.) Next, and critically, we seek out a professor on campus who is already committed to the curriculum to spearhead the program. That is one reason so many scholars in political theory or political thought are associated with our project. They have dedicated their lives to the study and teaching of the great ideas that shape American political life. Thirdly, we offer financial assistance through our partner donors. And finally, the JMC staff works closely with the professors and the universities to make sure the programs are successful.

As a result of all of this, we currently have about nine hundred professors on over three hundred campuses across the country and we are expanding every year. We also are positioned, and have begun to use this network of professors and colleges to set up high school teachers' academies across the country, so that the teaching of American principles and history starts at the high school level.

8

A SPUR-OF-THE-MOMENT START

In 2004, several people from a non-profit organization I had been supporting, which was working at the college level to promote the concept of liberty, came to my office and asked me if I would increase my support. I had recently read an article that reported that many political science and history professors on college campuses who had been radical student protestors in the 1960s had eliminated courses on America's founding principles and history at their universities. So, on the spur of the moment, I told these folks that I would give them a hell of a lot more than they were asking for if they would start a program to reintroduce these courses into the curricula.

While it seemed to be a spur-of-the-moment decision to start this initiative, I realize now that this was really the culmination of a lifetime of experience. It was the coming together of growing up in the 1940s and 1950s, when patriotism was in the air, along with my experience of living the American dream—realizing what our Founders meant when they spoke of the Pursuit of Happiness, the improving of one's position in life. All my years of being responsible for myself, of being responsible for the consequences of my actions, brought me to this decision.

I lived what America used to be about. And I am truly sad as I see it drifting further and further away from the principles that made it so unique and that helped make it so successful, and such a wonderful place to live. But after we sold the business and I had more time, I began to notice how much our country had changed. It was almost as if I were a modern-day Rip Van Winkle and had just awakened from a seventy-year sleep, and I didn't like what this changed America looked like.

I agreed to fund this program, committing several million dollars to the start-up. Several years later, in 2007, I realized the opportunities were so great that I decided to start a separate 501(c)(3) organization that would focus like a laser beam on our unique vision.

This was the beginning of one of the most interesting and exciting things I have ever done.

Today, fourteen years since the start of the project and tens of millions of dollars later, in addition to even more donations from others, the Jack Miller Center for Teaching America's Founding Principles and History has become a huge success. We have over nine hundred professors in our network on three hundred campuses across the country and we have the potential to expand our reach for many years to come. Our goal, working in partnership with professors, administrators, and other donors, is to enrich higher education and to give millions of students the opportunity they otherwise would not have to learn about and appreciate our nation's founding principles and history.

The most exciting part of it is that we are introducing a whole new field of study, American Constitutionalism, into higher education. This study reaches across disciplinary boundaries to include specialists in political theory and political thought, intellectual and cultural history, constitutional law, political economy, and classics. At several universities it is even becoming a separate department or school, while at others it is becoming a separate field of study within the Political Science departments. Of course, at most colleges and universities, we simply have for-credit courses in American political thought taught by one or more of the professors from the over nine hundred who, as part of our community, are working to advance education in America's founding principles and history.

All of this didn't just happen out of nowhere. It is the result of a carefully planned and well-executed strategy supporting a very clear mission statement. I was fortunate that the three people who had been working on it from the start, Retired Rear Admiral Mike Ratliff, Professor Mike Andrews, and Mike Deshaies, all agreed to join me in the new entity, on the condition that I would agree to a five-year funding plan to provide them with the time and opportunity to make it successful. I agreed to do so, and it has proven to be one of the most successful philanthropic investments I have ever made.

When we first started within the other organization back in 2004, we called together fifty professors in this field from around the country, and from various types of colleges and universities. The two-day meeting, which took place in a Chicago hotel, was filled with gloom and doom.

"It can't be done." "Other professors will fight it." "The administration won't support it." This was the common feeling. When we asked what problems they faced, they almost universally said, "Money, and help with the administrators and with curricula." As we kept asking questions and probing the situation, we soon had the walls of the room filled with big poster-sized sheets of paper full of ideas and roadblocks. It is from those ideas and comments that we began to develop a strategy.

It reminded me a lot of that comment I heard when I first started Quill. A vice president at my supplier, United Stationers, said, "Why do you want to start an office supply company? There are already 150 in Chicago." Well, despite all the competition already in place, I started the company, and we became one of the largest office products companies in the country. So these comments weren't going to deter me. After the meeting was over and everyone went home, we developed a plan using everything we had learned from the meeting.

Over the past fourteen years that plan has been refined and expanded, but never basically changed. And these days, when we have meetings of professors from various universities, they express tremendous enthusiasm and optimism. You never hear anyone say, "It can never be done." We hear tremendous appreciation for what we have done in the past and are doing still, and tales of the success our professors are having on their campuses. So how did that come about?

Again, I give a lot of credit to the people we put in charge, and to the many more we have added to the staff. Their great ability and wide knowledge of the field, combined with their tremendous enthusiasm for what we are doing, really are making it happen. My multiyear, multimillion-dollar commitment gave them the assurance they needed when we decided in 2007 to become a separate 501(c)(3) organization with a highly focused mission—to teach American founding principles and history to our young people. We focused solely on the college and university level, but more recently we have begun to reach out to the high school level with training programs for social studies teachers.

But what also helped tremendously was that we have set up the organization on a businesslike basis, running it like a business, using many of the principles I learned running Quill so successfully, principles I talk about in my book, *Simply Success: How to Start, Build and Grow a Multimillion Dollar Business—the Old-Fashioned Way* (Miller 2008).

Donor's intent has become our sacred commandment. For people who want to donate money to schools of their choice for this purpose, we have become by far and away the best stewards of their money to assure maximum results in meeting their expectations in this area, bar none. Before accepting their money, we carefully research the school and its faculty. In several instances, we have advised the potential donors not to waste their money. Their alma mater, we have said, will never stick with this mission.

In *Simply Success,* I spend an entire chapter on "The Magic of a Vision" (Miller 2008, 5360). A clearly defined, well-thought-out vision is what guides every subsequent action you take. It becomes your North Star. As I said at the beginning of this book, the vision of the United States is in the American Declaration of Independence, "that all Men are created equal, that they are endowed by their Creator with certain unalienable Rights and that among these are Life, Liberty, and the Pursuit of Happiness." Everything we Americans do as a country should be guided by that vision statement. Our vision for the Miller Center was to reintroduce into our schools the teaching of America's vision and the form of government our Founders established to realize it. My hope is that this will be my legacy to the country.

Today we have twelve full-time employees in our headquarters in Philadelphia, coordinating with dozens of professors who lead programs on campuses from Boston to Atlanta, from South Bend, Indiana, to Texas and from Virginia to Portland, Oregon. Also, hundreds of donors are now helping to support the JMC's academic programs and efforts on campuses across the country.

9

THE PROFESSORS ARE THE KEY TO SUCCESS

The professors are the engines of change on college campuses. So we focus on identifying those who are committed to a lifetime of teaching and who share our mission. Our job is to build a community of professors who will teach the philosophical basis of American founding principles, who will teach the principles and the history of our country as it has progressed toward actualizing them. We do this in many ways, from funding the Summer Institutes to supporting the professors in their careers and in their efforts on campus. With the help of hundreds of other donors, we are able both to provide start-up support and to work to find them the additional support they will need to fully realize their potential.

We recognize that we have to fill up the pipeline with more young scholars who are committed to this effort. We work closely with the JMC's Academic Advisory Council, which includes many of the nation's leading senior political scientists and historians, to identify talented young scholars and help them get on a path that leads to tenure track positions. The Miller Postdoctoral Fellowship program is an essential part of this effort, as it provides valuable teaching and research experience that is so helpful in a tight job market in the fields of political science and history.

Our Summer Institutes, which are modeled after a program run by Professor Robert George at Princeton, are our most important programs: they serve as the entry point for young scholars into the Miller network. The Institutes, held in partnership with leading universities, are attended by twenty to twenty-five young and early-career scholars who spend ten days studying and discussing the original texts that became the basis of our nation's Founding.

In these ten days, young scholars meet and get to know others with common intellectual interests. They also have the rare opportunity to study with some of the most renowned professors in the field.

They come away not only with a great deal more knowledge, but also with a network of friends they can lean on and exchange ideas with through the years. For the past fourteen years we have held such Institutes each summer. Goldie and I have attended the last two or three days of each of these past twenty-five Summer Institutes, and they have been some of the greatest, most rewarding experiences we have ever had, in addition to being, for me, the best liberal arts education possible.

The young scholars we meet are amazing. They are already well-versed in their fields of study. For the Summer Institute discussions they each receive a reader that includes a few hundred pages of documents from the Ancient Greeks and Romans up to the Founding of the American republic and beyond. I always get the readings well in advance and make sure I read everything that is going to be discussed while we are there.

Then I attend the seminars and take a very active part in the discussions. The scholars are a heck of a lot smarter, academically, and better read than I am, but I find that my practical, real world experience helps me bring something different to their sometimes esoteric discussions.

And, over the years, getting to know many of our nation's leading professors in political science and history, like Jim Ceaser at the University of Virginia and Bill McClay at the University of Oklahoma, both of whom are co-chairs of our Academic Advisory Council, has been very rewarding. These are people who have been teaching, researching, and writing on the American Founding and history for many years. They are among the best in the field. So to engage with them during the seminars, or at lunch or dinner or over a drink, is a real treat as well as a great learning experience. The after-dinner lectures featuring prominent public intellectuals are an added bonus.

While we are attending these seminars, we always hear rave reviews from the young scholars. "Best learning experience I ever had." "Wow, I always felt so 'alone' on campus, but now I have friends I can talk to about this." "I have gone to other programs, but this is by far the best ever." And best of all, they profusely thank Goldie and me for everything we are doing to help them in their careers. These are some of the most dedicated young people I have ever met.

At the Institute's concluding dinner, Goldie and I make a few comments. Mine can usually be summarized as, "You thank us for what we are doing for you, but we want to thank you for what you are going to do as you go out and teach our young people the principles that have made this country of ours so great, so unique." Goldie's comments usually include something like, "You've had ten days of free food, free booze, and good conversation. But there is no free lunch. Now you have to go out and work hard to teach your students what a great country we have."

Our Summer Institutes are achieving what we had hoped for, providing hundreds of young scholars who are committed to a lifetime of teaching American founding principles and history a pathway to jobs on campuses across our country.

Another essential element of the Miller Center is the service we provide to donors who want to provide funding to start an academic center of excellence at their alma mater. Thanks to the large nationwide network of established scholars and the research provided by the Miller Center staff of former college professors, we are able to identify faculty who share our mission and who want to further this curriculum.

10

A FULL-FLEDGED PROGRAM HELPS ASSURE SUCCESS

One of the most critical requirements for a young professor to get a tenure-track position is to get published. Early on in our project, we realized that publishing opportunities for scholars specializing in the Founding were almost nonexistent. One night, after dinner at a Miller Center event, I was sitting around with some of the Miller Center people and a few professors, talking about this problem. I hadn't heard about it before but after they explained it to me, I said, in my usual charge-ahead way, "Hell, let's just publish our own journal."

A year and a half later, in 2012, *American Political Thought: A Journal of Ideas, Institutions, and Culture* was published. It is edited by one of America's premier scholars in the field, Professor Michael Zuckert at the University of Notre Dame, and published by the University of Chicago Press. It's a top-quality, peer-reviewed journal. It started as a semiannual publication and is now published quarterly. It is even making a profit. You can find it in many university libraries across the country and it also has many individual subscribers.

Notre Dame thought the journal was so important that they relieved Professor Zuckert of many of his teaching duties and provided him with an office and an assistant so he could focus on the journal. Professor Zuckert had built up a strong faculty in his department, so the teaching of American political thought continued at Notre Dame while he edited the journal.

At the same time, political theorists who had become part of JMC's national community of professors working to advance education in American founding principles asked our Center to help establish a home for scholars working in American political thought within the American Political Science Association (APSA). This has led to an organized section within the APSA that offers young professors who are concerned with education in America's founding principles greatly increased opportunities to advance their careers. This growing interest in the study and teaching of American political thought and Constitutional Studies has led to thousands of new and revised courses to meet student interest in this field. It has been exciting to see new certificate programs that meet undergraduate requirements for graduation and new minor fields of study or concentrations in Constitutionalism emerge on campuses, such as: the minor and/or certificate in American Constitutional Democracy through the Kinder Institute on Constitutional Democracy at the University of Missouri; the Constitutional Studies minor at Notre Dame; the certificate in Core Texts and Ideas at the Thomas Jefferson Center at the University of Texas at Austin; and the Constitutional Studies concentration at Christopher Newport University in Virginia. This is one more part of a multipronged effort to enrich the programs currently offered on campuses for the teaching of America's founding principles and history.

We have also set up partnerships with some of the leading research libraries in the country: the Newberry Library in Chicago, the Huntington Library in San Marino, California, the John D. Rockefeller Jr. Library in Colonial Williamsburg, Virginia, and the American Philosophical Society in Philadelphia. In collaboration with these topflight research libraries, with their unparalleled collection of documents and manuscripts from the founding era, our early- and mid-career professors can study and write while conducting research in rare collections of original historical documents. The young scholars chosen for these fellowships have an unusual opportunity not only to further their careers but also to deepen their understanding of the sources and ideas that have shaped our country and form of government. Donations to the Miller Center make these fellowships possible.

In addition, thanks to a $1 million gift from an anonymous donor and additional money from other donors, we established a Miller Center Postdoctoral Fellowship program. To date, 163 fellowships for one- to three-year appointments have been awarded to promising young scholars in the field. These fellowships, which are supplemented by funding from the host universities, are very important for these young scholars as they build not only their teaching credentials but also their publishing record. We will continue to award many more in the future.

Each fellowship costs approximately $50,000 for a year, which then turns into about $4 million of lifetime value per professor. Not a bad investment! These postdoctoral fellowships go to promising scholars who have their PhD, but do not yet have a job. At MIT, for example, the postdoc both teaches courses and assists Professor Bernhardt Trout, director of the MIT Benjamin Franklin Project, with program administration. At the University of Pennsylvania's Program on Democracy, Citizenship, and Constitutionalism, Professor Rogers Smith, a regular facilitator in our Philadelphia-based Summer Institutes, received support for a scholar to focus on American Constitutionalism.

These fellowships, which are sponsored by our partner programs directed by professors in the Miller community, advance the careers of the young postdocs, provide education that would otherwise be unavailable to the students on their campuses, and enhance the importance of the partner programs. Each postdoc goes through a rigorous vetting process to ensure that those with the most potential receive the fellowships.

Finally, to build upon this success, we have established a program of three-day refresher courses for our most promising young scholars, those who have shown an entrepreneurial spirit in building new programs on American political thought and the Founding on their own campuses. These refresher courses not only bring new ideas and insights to the field, but they also strengthen the bonds between our young faculty partners.

The staff of former college professors at the Miller Center have developed an extraordinary process for recruiting, motivating, and networking young professors, in addition to helping them get their first jobs and advance their careers. As they secure tenure-track positions and prove their worth as scholars and teachers, we provide guidance and other help, particularly to those who want to start a Miller partner program on their campus. As a result, a strong cadre of professors has been built who will enrich the teaching of American founding principles on campuses across the country for many decades to come. Almost nine hundred thousand students have already taken courses offered by members of our community of professors dedicated to advancing education in America's founding principles and history. Over time, many millions of students will benefit from teaching by our Miller faculty partners.

This is the foundation on which all else will come, and we will continue to build and strengthen this foundation. This is what excites me the most about our program: these young scholars, every one of whom I have met at least once over the past fourteen years, and more of whom I hope to meet in the years ahead, will be the engine that will drive the effort to reinvigorate this essential field of study.

Building the community of professors was just part of the challenge of getting the teaching of American founding principles back into university curricula. The second part was working with the universities and colleges themselves. But this wasn't as difficult as our professors at that first meeting in Chicago said it would be.

And this, we believe, was due to our approach. The Jack Miller Center was established as a nonsectarian and nonpartisan project. We are not ideological—beyond representing the ideas on which the Founders established our country. Further, there is no Jack Miller Curriculum. Instead, we seek out teachers and professors who share our commitment to a profound education in America's founding principles and history and, whenever possible, provide any help they ask of us, and then we let them do their job.

When I started the Miller Center, Mike Ratliff, Mike Andrews, Mike Deshaies, and I decided that our approach would be to work with the universities to fill this vacuum in their curriculum offerings. We determined to be neither partisan nor sectarian. Also—and this is crucial—we approached each university with the proposition that we wanted to enrich the educational opportunities they were offering their students. In other words, we didn't want to come in and radically change what they were doing. We simply wanted to add to it, to enrich it. In addition, we offered to help support our young professors during their first few years of teaching, offsetting costs the universities would otherwise need to pay. At a time when state and federal funding was running short, this was a very welcome offer.

With this approach, we now have professors teaching on some three hundred campuses to date, with more starting up every year. Our faculty partner professors are on campuses across the country, including elite universities such as Yale, Columbia, Harvard, MIT, Notre Dame, and Northwestern, and flagship state universities such as the University of Texas, the University of Missouri, the University of Wisconsin, and the University of Virginia, as well as smaller leading liberal arts colleges such as Carthage and Rhodes.

We begin by seeking out professors on campus who share our mission. We invite them to a Miller Summer Institute, where we get to know them well and where they can learn about our project. If there is potential for a successful partnership, we, along with the faculty partner, reach out to the college's administration. Once we have all parties fully informed and on board with the mission, then—and only then—do we proceed to establish a program on that campus. We want to make absolutely certain that there will be the greatest opportunity for success, that the donor's money will be wisely used, and that the donor's intent will be carefully followed.

Finally, there are programs that are national in scope that help promote the work we do and that also provide a support network for the JMC circle of scholars. The first of these is our memberships in the professional associations many of our professors already belong to—the APSA, for example, which holds conferences where we help facilitate panels and discussions. Also, we take advantage of these gatherings to have special cocktail receptions before or after the official business of the conferences to give our scholars another opportunity to bond and exchange ideas and experiences.

The Constitution Day Initiative is another national program the Miller Center has undertaken. In 2004, Congress passed a law mandating that all federally funded educational institutions must provide programs on the Constitution on or near September 17, which is Constitution Day. This mandate has been basically ignored or given only token attention. So, we launched our own Constitution Day Initiative in 2011, with a generous lead gift from the Andrea Waitt Carlton Family Foundation. The JMC faculty partners compete for funding that we provide to conduct programs on Constitution Day. Some of our nation's leading scholars, public intellectuals, and legal experts, including the late Supreme Court Justice Antonin Scalia, have participated in Constitution Day programs that we have supported. In addition, JMC faculty partners have published essays about the Constitution in leading newspapers and online websites. We are continuing to perfect this program and to expand it to more and more campuses every year.

Then, each year in Philadelphia, we gather together forty to fifty professors to discuss what is happening in higher education and how we can improve the role we play in it. The participants represent a cross-section of colleges and universities. This summit continues to give us fresh insights on how we can improve and how we can best serve both the professors and the schools. It helps keep us at the forefront of what is happening in higher education. Along with other Jack Miller Center Directors, I have attended dinners, luncheons, and panels at these summits and find them a great resource for ideas.

We are also developing an online presence. We have a very strong website, jackmillercenter.org, where we provide a lot of information about our mission and programs and a tremendous trove of relevant material. This spans the entire spectrum of listings and reviews of the best books on subjects related to the Founding, as well as many excellent videos of lectures given by the best scholars in the field, covering topics from freedom to the meaning of the Pursuit of Happiness, the rule of law, and the whole range of subjects, so that anyone who is interested, from students to retirees, can learn from the best. And this reservoir of material keeps expanding. One day we hope to be the go-to source for information in American political thought.

In conclusion, as we continue to build this ever-expanding cadre of topflight scholars in Constitutionalism and American political thought, and to support the professors and their efforts, we will also continue to build a special *esprit de corps* among them so they will enthusiastically teach that spirit of freedom and liberty that our Founders intended for our country, the spirit needed if our people are to become informed and participating citizens, and not simply subjects. These scholars then become the engine to spread this teaching to other areas, such as to the high schools.

11

EXPANDING OUR
MISSION TO
HIGH SCHOOLS

For some time now I have felt that our efforts aren't enough. We need to start earlier, in the high schools, so that students going on to college will be prepared for a deeper study in this area. And many donors I have spoken with have said the same thing. A few years ago, we made a halfhearted effort to start such a program but, although the high school teachers loved it, it went nowhere. So, after two years, we gave it up.

However, the idea kept nagging at me, and in 2016 I made Mike Ratliff an offer to pay the salary of one JMC staff member to start a high school initiative and focus on it to the exclusion of any other tasks. My brother Harvey stepped up with a very generous offer to fund all the other expenses for a three-year start-up program. In 2015, my home state of Illinois passed a law that requires every student to take a course in civics in order to graduate from high school. I thought this would be a great opportunity to get the teaching of American founding principles and history into every school in the state.

When we tried it before, we gave the assignment to someone who was already busy working on our university program, spending most of her time travelling to campuses around the country. From my experience at Quill, I knew that, if we were to succeed, we needed someone whose only job was to lead this effort, someone who would live or die with the success of the effort.

The Miller Center had just rehired a young man, Tom Kelly, who had left the Miller Center several years before to go to law school. After working at a law firm, Tom realized that he liked what was going on at the Miller Center better than being a lawyer. He enthusiastically accepted the challenge and started working on the high school initiative.

The plan was to start with a pilot program in Chicago, my hometown, and if that proved successful, to expand it to other parts of the country. We knew we couldn't teach the students directly because there are just too many of them, and they keep changing with each new school year. The best approach was to train the teachers so they could then teach their students year after year. So Tom created a program with that approach.

High schools work differently than universities. At the university level, the professors pretty much determine what is taught and so your entry is through them. But at the high school level, the administrators determine what is taught. The new law in Illinois about teaching civics had no provisions for what civics meant. To many people, civic education means encouraging young people to do volunteer community work. Others might interpret it differently. Our challenge was to make sure it meant teaching the principles and practices and history of the American experiment in self-government so our young people can learn how to become good, informed citizens.

The administrators Tom met with were all enthusiastic about what we wanted to do. On one visit, an administrator even told us that the district had money in their budget to pay for teacher training courses, which was great to hear. During our first attempt, a few years earlier, we paid teachers to attend, something I opposed then and wouldn't agree to this time.

But if we weren't going to pay them to use their free time to attend classes, what might we offer teachers that would help them in their teaching and add value to this education? Tom worked with several universities in the area and came up with a plan for the teachers to get the state-required teaching credits and the option of credit toward a master's degree. A master's degree would mean a hike in their salary level. Tom developed the curriculum, working with others at the Miller Center and some of the professors in our group. With all of this in place, we needed a good location to hold the classes. We reached out to the Newberry Library, one of the premier research libraries in the country. We'd worked with the Newberry before. They have a good collection of founding documents as well as a high school teachers' initiative of their own. They welcomed the opportunity to also be a part of our program.

The Miller Center is in a unique position to make a success of this program because we have so many qualified professors around the country who can work in their local communities and, with our help, make it happen. Some of our professors had already begun such programs themselves in their communities.

So, starting in 2016, we began a serious high school teachers' initiative with Chicago as the proving ground. With three distinct programs, from classroom to online to a combination of both, high school teachers will get a solid intellectual background on American founding principles and history that will enrich their teaching of these subjects for many years to come.

As this program proves itself and is perfected, we will expand into other areas of the country. As we see it, we are the only organization in the country who can make this a successful national program because of our nationwide network of professors who are available and eager to teach the subject. We focus on teaching the teachers content, not more teaching techniques.

To develop this into a full-blown national program, the only other thing we need are donors who are willing to support programs in their communities. With so many people anxious to help improve education at the high school level, this should not be a problem.

So the Jack Miller Center is now growing into a powerful force to help improve the civic education our young people receive at both the university and the high school levels. Our overarching goal is to provide students with the best education possible to prepare them to be good stewards of the free institutions of our nation that protect all Americans' liberties.

HELPING DONORS
INVEST WISELY

Another essential component of our culture at the Miller Center is the service and integrity we provide donors who are truly interested in enriching the educational experience our young people get in the area of American political thought and American history.

As a philanthropist myself, I know the disappointment and frustration you feel when you find your money isn't being used wisely, or worse yet, when it is not used for the purpose for which you donated. So we have made it an absolute, rock-solid commitment at the Miller Center to always observe donors' intent and to be extraordinarily careful about how a donor's money is invested. We look on ourselves as the stewards of the donors' funds. Most of our donors are passionate about getting the teaching of American founding principles and history back into the schools. We are making that happen, and with enough support, we can help reestablish it once again as a basic part of the school experience.

A few examples might help explain what I mean. Normally, when a donor gives to a university for a particular cause, the university takes a huge amount, often twenty-five to fifty percent, for operating costs. As a non-profit, with a policy of not paying overhead, only in rare circumstances do we ever agree to make an exception and pay these charges. Indeed, since we are responding in all cases to a request for help from the university, we expect that the campus will itself contribute to the project, which we approach as a partnership. Often, that is in the form of in-kind support, such as office space, or personnel. The successful partnership between the Kinder Family Foundation and the University of Missouri set a new national standard in support for liberal studies when the campus agreed to a cash match to the Kinder's support for establishing what is the most important new program, at any American Association of Universities (AAU) campus, related to the study and teaching of America's founding principles and history. Other precedent-setting funding arrangements at the University of Virginia, Carthage College, Christopher Newport University, and Notre Dame University have resulted in significant new resources being directed to advance teaching that will prepare students to be better citizens.

Also, many non-profit organizations seem to have needs that outstrip their resources, so they often commit to projects, whether buildings or programs, before having the money in place. They are then under tremendous pressure to raise the money. Or there are programs that are deemed critical, which they can't move forward on without the funding. They often get partial funding, start moving forward, and then are desperate for more funding. At the Miller Center, we don't undertake an effort until the funding is in place.

Another example of how we protect the donor's intent is the care we take in making sure the donors' money will be used as they intended. We have an individual on staff who is responsible for investigating the receptivity of certain universities to our programs. In several instances, we have advised donors to *not* invest money in their alma mater for our type of program because their investment would almost surely be diverted in some fashion. For example, if they wanted a program on American history, the university would offer a course with that title, but then would hire a professor who would teach it through the lens of slavery, women's oppression, and class warfare.

Those subjects are a part of the American experience, and they have a role in the study and teaching of American history on our campuses. But a profound and balanced curriculum must offer survey courses that give students the full story, and provide space on their faculty and in their course catalogue for the exploration of that fuller, balanced story. Like all ancient states, Athens was a slave state. But Athenians changed history by becoming the first society to adopt democratic institutions. Locke and Montesquieu were part of monarchical societies, and Monroe and Jefferson owned slaves, but we study them because of their contributions to an intellectual tradition that opened the way for a republican government that has dramatically expanded the scope of human freedom. Our greatest scholars understand this and place their emphasis on what is most important and most remarkable in the American story.

The University of Pennsylvania's Walter McDougall begins his book *Freedom Just Around the Corner* by reminding us that history has changed fundamentally since 1500 because of one thing: the emergence of the American republic, with its new political and economic arrangements (McDougall 2004).

Akhil Amar of the Yale Law School began his keynote remarks at the JMC's 2016 Constitution Day programs by dividing history between "BC" ("Before the Constitution") and "AD" ("After the Document"). He described the U.S. Constitution as "the hinge of human history, of modern history" because, after 1789, "nothing was the same" (Amar 2016). American students also need to learn about the continuing struggle to more perfectly realize the ideals of the Declaration of Independence embodied in the American experiment in liberty.

Finally, a word about non-restricted funds and endowments. Most donors like to give for specific programs and—in this field—to their alma maters or other specific schools, and that is fine. But as I mention later in the book, after my wife and I got married, we joined a Synagogue so one would be there when we needed it. The same is true when giving to an organization that is working for a cause you believe in.

From the beginning, I have basically supported the Miller Center by covering its operating costs. And I have provided for the Miller Center in my estate planning. However, it has now grown too large for me to continue to support the operations by myself. In order to continue the success of our work to provide students with an education in America's founding principles and history, one way that we have been helping to resolve this problem is by charging those who donate for specific programs for the direct costs we incur, labor and otherwise, for implementing those programs. I believe a small surcharge on top of that would be prudent. In addition, future fundraising must emphasize the importance of non-restricted funds to support our Summer Institutes and other programs that are essential to our cause.

Finally, it is critical to build a strong endowment fund to guarantee the sustainability of the Miller Center. Just fourteen years into this effort, we have proven that we can reverse the decline in the teaching of the founding principles and history to our young people. We can instill in them the love of freedom, hard work, self-reliance and so much more that are the ingredients of the culture that has made America so exceptional, so great. And as I have said earlier in the book, like the statue of the self-made man in my office, this is not a job we can finish, but neither is it something we can desist from working at. After all, as President Reagan said, "Freedom is never more than one generation away from extinction." Our mission is to make sure that every generation learns and understands what it is in America that preserves that freedom.

Retired Rear Admiral Michael Ratliff (right) was president of the Jack Miller Center from its inception until 2018. He is seen here in discussions with Dr. Michael Andrews, his successor, who has also been with the Miller Center since its founding. *Source: Jack Miller Center*

The Jack Miller Center Board of Directors, 2017. *Source: Jim Roese Photography*

Constitution Day—The Jack Miller Center has made it a mission to make Constitution Day, September 17th, become a stronger event on campuses as mandated by Congress on April 15, 1957. *Source: Tony Tribble Photography*

High school teachers hard at work at the Jack Miller Center High School Teachers Institute. *Source: Jim Summaria Photography*

The Jack Miller Center's new High School Teachers program is beginning to grow. *Source: Freedom & Citizenship at Center for American Studies*

I'm hard at work during a JMC Summer Institute session. *Source: Jim Roese Photography*

Summer Institute professors with Goldie, me, and the staff–Pasadena CA, 2015. *Source: Jim Roese Photography*

Conversation at a Summer Institute dinner. *Source: Andrew Shurtleff Photography*

Professors at the Summer Institute. *Source: Jim Roese Photography*

Discussing the Founding, a favorite subject. *Source: Jim Summaria*

A LIFE WELL LIVED

What Can Happen When One Uses Hard Work and Determination to Take Advantage of What a Free Society Makes Possible

It might seem odd to include my life story as part of a book on the founding principles, but it is here for a reason. It is here because my story is representative of so many other stories of people who were fortunate enough to be born in the United States, or who came here to enjoy the freedoms we have because of the type of government and the principles our Founders gave us.

Mine is a story of a quite ordinary guy who, as a result of a strong focus and a lot of hard work, was able to realize the American dream because he was free to do so without excessive government interference. It's a dream so many others have also achieved to a greater or lesser extent, consistent with their potential and effort.

So I present my story simply as being representative of what can be achieved in a free society based on a free-market economy. Nothing more and nothing less.

13

GROWING UP IN A PATRIOTIC AMERICA

L ife, it seems to me, is a series of events, big or small, that can change your direction forever. I don't believe we have much control over the events, but we can control our reaction to them. I have a quote on a small plaque on my dresser that captures that thought: "You can't control the winds, but you can adjust the sails."

If Nicholas II, the last Tsar of Russia, and the Cossacks had not been so anti-Semitic, my grandparents might not have chosen to leave Russia at the beginning of the 1900s and come to America. My parents wouldn't have met and I wouldn't have been born. But all that happened, and I was born in Chicago on March 19, 1929, the second son of Ben and Ida Miller.

I don't remember much about the first six or seven years of my life except my Dad chasing a burglar out of our first-floor apartment one night with nothing but a tennis racquet in hand, and my older brother, Arnold, getting an infection that resulted in eleven operations in the course of four years spent in and out of hospitals. I don't remember anything about my first few years in school.

Then we moved to a new neighborhood, Albany Park, on the Northwest Side of Chicago. That put me into a new grade school, Hibbard, and into a class with someone named Howard Bernstein, who would become a lifelong friend and my partner in a hand-balancing act. It also put me into the district for Von Steuben High School, which had a great impact on my life.

And what a great time to be growing up! We roamed the neighborhood on our balloon-tired Schwinn bikes at all hours of the day and night, just so we were home for meals and bedtime. As I remember it, the teachers were strict, and we didn't dare break the rules—well, at least, not often, and not openly, and not without consequences. But we still had a lot of fun. Before we got our drivers' licenses when we were fifteen, taking a streetcar and then a bus for a day at Montrose Beach was a weekend summer ritual. It was a tremendous freedom just to be kids. There wasn't the fear that seems to be forcing even suburban parents to take their kids everywhere, protecting them from all dangers. And we didn't have a lot of organized activities to keep us busy. We just sort of hung out and organized our own baseball games and other activities.

Also, it was an exciting time to be growing up. I was in grade school and high school during the Second World War. I have strong memories of the excitement and patriotism that were in the air. On Saturdays, Mom would give us twenty-five cents to go to the movies. Thanks to the newsreels, we saw the war right there on the big screen, the invasions, and the battles at sea, our planes bombing the German cities, the dogfights in the air, all of it.

Every Sunday evening, the family would sit around the radio listening to Walter Winchell, who would begin every news broadcast in his breathless way, "Good evening, Mr. and Mrs. America, and all the ships at sea." With rapid-fire words and the bursts of the sound of a telegraph key, he would then deliver the latest war news. Funny, the things you remember.

But what a great time to be an American! We were proud of our country, proud of the all-out effort to win the war and proud of the bravery of our fighting men.

We saved tinfoil from chewing gum and cigarette packages and rolled it up into big baseball-size balls to donate to the war effort. And, of course, there was gas rationing. Dad had a "C" sticker, which meant he could get just three gallons of gas a week. Three gallons didn't go very far, so for dates we had to scrounge for someone's unused stickers. In a desperate situation, there was a gas station on Foster Avenue across the street from a police station that sold black market gas at a much higher price.

My high school days were the greatest I could have asked for and they played a major role in what happened in the rest of my life. To this day, my closest friends are from my high school, not my college days. Also, it was during high school that I got in with a group of serious students who influenced me a great deal.

Most people I know identify with their college days, not their high school days. For me it's the opposite. College was just a blur, something I wanted to get through as fast as I could. It was just work, study, and heavy class loads so I could graduate in three and a half years with no debt. I carried nineteen hours a semester, when fifteen was a normal load. I took almost all business classes and don't remember taking a single liberal arts class, something I now regret.

High school was the place that really set me on the right course, at least the last two years of it. After the first year at Von, for some reason I decided to transfer to Lane Tech. From that experience, I remember making a set of twenty-five-pound barbell weights in foundry class and being slapped by an instructor when I refused to get into the pool one day when I was sick. That slap helped me decide to transfer back to Von. Also, I don't remember taking a single course in American history or our founding principles at either Lane Tech or Von Steuben. I can see now that this left a big gap in my education.

When I was thirteen and just starting high school, four or five of us pooled some money, nineteen dollars or so, and ordered a set of weights from the York Barbell Company in York, Pennsylvania. And so began a life-long habit, seventy-five years so far, of working out. We started in an unheated garage. Later I used my basements and now I have a fully equipped gym in the house.

When I transferred back to Von in my junior year, my friend Howard Bernstein and I began doing some gymnastics and also playing around with hand-balancing, practicing during the gym periods while most of the other kids played basketball. Throughout my life, I chose the individual, not team, activities. They included weightlifting, hand-balancing, handball (thirty-five years of it), tennis, and then golf, after my knees and neck gave out.

We worked hard on the hand-balancing, and while we were still in high school, we became good enough to enter a talent show on TV, which was in its early stages then. We won and received a prize of a full-console, ten-inch, black-and-white TV set. Since Howard's family already had one, I bought his half, and so our family had our first TV set. I remember Dad lying on the floor, his head cradled in his hand, watching the professional wrestling matches, cheering his favorites, and complaining when he felt the referees made a bad call.

We performed at the beach to impress the girls and later, during college, performed at a few county fairs in Illinois, Iowa, and Ohio, and at some social clubs. We never made it into the big time, but we made a little money and had a lot of fun. Even after we graduated from college we kept it up for a while.

It was during my high school days that my Dad's life changed dramatically, a change that affected me and my thinking to this day. For years, Dad had worked at the Metropolitan Life Insurance Company, working his way up from salesman on what was called a debit, to assistant manager, and then to being the youngest manager in the Metropolitan's history at that time. It was a good job with great security and good pay.

But managers were not supposed to own an outside business, and Dad had bought one, which included two live poultry stores, one on the Northwest Side of Chicago and the other on Sheffield Avenue, a block from Wrigley Field, home of the Chicago Cubs. He bought them to help his brother, Abe, who was having trouble finding a job and, of course, he bought them as an investment.

Later, after they sold the stores, Abe ended up working at our company, Quill, where he enjoyed the best, most secure period in his life. But Dad was fired as a result of the purchase. After a year of trying to find a position commensurate with his position and pay at the Metropolitan, he hung up his suits, put on khakis and an apron, and began to run the Sheffield store.

What a step down! Out of embarrassment, I suppose, Dad stopped seeing his former friends, the other managers at the Metropolitan. Mom, who hadn't worked since she had given birth to Arnold, got a job at a downtown department store to help out with the expenses. To their credit, I never heard a complaint from either one of them. They just did what they had to do. As I thought about this in recent years, my pride in them grew a great deal.

To make things worse, Dad bought the live poultry stores at the same time the grocery chains started pushing chicken and chicken parts at prices far below the prices Dad could afford to ask. Also, the immigrant women who would come into the store and personally pick out the bird they wanted just before it was slaughtered were becoming a disappearing group. Dad held on for a number of years, managing to get by. But there were many times when I would get home late from a date and, as I passed their bedroom, I could see Dad lying in bed on his side, with his head propped up on his bent arm, wide awake, worrying.

I vowed that would never happen to me. In the good times, Dad had always been a happy-go-lucky kind of a guy. He never saved very much, feeling "there was more where that came from." I remember once, in the good days, when he gave me a ten-dollar bill, which in 1945 was equivalent to $135 in 2017, to buy something at the store. I lost it on the way. Mom was very upset, but Dad just gave me more money and sent me out again. So when Dad hit that rough spot in his life and I saw how hard it was for him, I vowed I would work hard to make a lot of money and that I would be very careful how I spent it. To this day that habit stays with me, which is hard for Goldie to understand, since now I don't have to be that careful. But I still go around turning off lights to save on electricity. Habits die hard.

But to get back to Von. In those days, it truly was a great school, with a lot of really smart kids and terrific teachers. For my first two years in high school my grades were okay, but not great. But when I transferred back to Von in my junior year, I joined a club, the Corsairs. All of the members were among the top students in the class. So I buckled down and managed to bring my grades up so that I graduated in the top five percent or so.

In our senior year at Von, a group of us petitioned the math teacher for an extra class on college algebra. Also, three or four of us asked the English teacher to teach us advanced English informally, in her office, during her break period. These days they call them Advanced Placement classes.

14

THE COLLEGE YEARS,
A BLUR

When Howard and I graduated, we went to the University of Illinois in Champaign. No one I knew ever thought of shopping around for out-of-state schools. The University of Illinois was right there. They had to take you if you had an Illinois high school diploma, and they were inexpensive. We both took and passed proficiency tests in college algebra and English, and started with six credit hours which, with the extra classes each semester, allowed us to graduate in just three-and-a-half years. So, as I have mentioned, we both decided to carry extra-heavy loads each semester, nineteen hours instead of the normal fifteen, so we could graduate in three-and-a-half years instead of the usual four, without going to summer school.

When I enrolled, my older brother, Arnold, still had a year or so to go in college and Dad, who already was stretched thin supporting him, couldn't afford to support both of us. So, I decided to pay my own way. I went down to Champaign with very little savings in my pocket and I knew I had to get a job right away. When I heard they needed people to sell subscriptions to the school paper, *The Daily Illini*, I immediately applied and got the job. This was about a week or so before school started, and I sold enough subscriptions to make about $136 (over $1,800 in 2017 dollars). Once the staff saw how much you could make selling subscriptions, they stopped letting non-staff members sell them. That was enough to help me get started. Then I got a job modeling for art classes, which paid a dollar an hour, more than most other jobs on campus paid.

Howard and I joined my brother's fraternity and lived in the frat house. But that lasted only about a year. I hated fraternity life—all the rules and regulations. And the last straw was one weekend when Howard had to go back to

Chicago. We had been assigned, as a pledge duty, to clean and straighten up the luggage room. Howard was gone, so I got up at 6:30 a.m. and by 9:30 or so I had the job done.

Almost everyone else was still sleeping. I grabbed a bite to eat, took my books, and went to a quiet place to study. When I returned that afternoon, I was confronted by the fraternity member who was in charge of pledge duties. He berated me for not staying to help the other pledges. I told him that I had done what both Howard and I were assigned to do. His reply was, "No, if you finish your assignment, you are supposed to help the other pledges." My reply to him was something like, "Screw you. I got up early and did ours while they were sleeping. I wasn't going to help them just because they wanted to sleep longer."

The next semester we left the fraternity—leaving, I think, before they could kick me out. I guess I didn't like a socialistic idea even then. Individual freedom and responsibility were part of my DNA from the beginning, so I suppose that's one reason I was so drawn to our founding principles later in life, with their emphasis on protecting the freedom of the individual.

In any event, I had given no thought to what I wanted to do in life, so I chose accounting because Howard's dad, whom I admired, was a CPA working for himself, and Howard was taking accounting. (He now brags that five of his grandchildren are CPAs, making it four generations of CPAs.) But after a year, I decided that wasn't for me and I switched to advertising. Then I ended up building a career and a business by mail order.

Looking back on it now, the most important thing I got from college that helped me in my career was, frankly, my courses in advertising, which sensitized me to the potential power in advertising. This was critical to the huge success we had at Quill. It always amazes me how small things, like switching to advertising, have such a huge impact on one's life. And you never know ahead of time what events or actions are going to have such an impact.

Also, now, as a result of my involvement with the Miller Center, I am truly sorry that I didn't take some liberal arts classes. I can't remember taking a single one. What I learned about business, I learned by working. This, by the way, makes me very leery about this tremendous push about everyone needing a college degree. That's nonsense. Some do, but others would be better off with apprenticeship training that would lead them on to good jobs, and perhaps even to starting a business of their own. And the country would be better off with a well-trained workforce.

My younger brother, Harvey, came down to Champaign in 1949 for his first year while I was in my last year. We roomed together in the men's residence, but for some reason, Harvey, who had been a very good student in high school, didn't like college and quit in the first year to join the Navy, where he served during the Korean War. His idealism, which he has a lot of, must have taken over. For me, the Korean War didn't stir any patriotic passions. It seemed far away, in a country I knew virtually nothing about, and I didn't understand why we were involved. It was not like World War II, which was much more personal.

Even though I had a heavy class load and work schedule, I still found time to practice our hand-balancing act, work out and study. My routine for studying was to read each day's assignment, underlining important items and thoughts. Then, before tests, I would study the underlined portions, and those I thought very important I would write on three-by-five index cards with a question on the other side. The night before an exam, I would go through the cards until I had memorized them all. For me, there was no late night cramming. I would be in bed by 10:30 even on the nights before an exam. Sort of boring, I guess, but it worked for me.

By the way, I never drank liquor in those days other than an occasional glass of beer and some wine at the Passover Seders. But one time, Howard and I decided to get drunk to see what it was like. So we each brought an acquaintance whose job it was to get us home, and we set out to get drunk.

After downing a number of glasses of Glueckstadt, a high-potency beer, I felt woozy, and Howard, who had an exam the next day, got sick and spent a good bit of the night in the bathroom. To this day, I have never been drunk. I just don't like the idea of not being in control of my actions. Today, when I read about the heavy drinking that goes on at college campuses I truly don't understand it—heavy drinking, some deaths, unwanted sexual encounters, the whole scene. Why supposedly smart people put themselves in those situations is beyond my understanding. I guess everyone is free to do what they want, so long as they accept the responsibility for what follows from their actions.

Also, because of my heavy schedule, I don't remember going to a single ball game. And dates were few and far between. In the late 1940s, returning GIs were flooding the campus. The boy-girl ratio was about seven to one, and the GI's were older and had more money. The girls often had four or five dates a weekend, usually with different guys, if you counted some lunches as dates. I couldn't afford the time or the money, and it wasn't worth the hassle.

During school, I modeled for a while and then got a job washing dishes at the men's residence where I lived. I made seventy-five cents an hour. In my last year, I was promoted to washing pots and pans in the kitchen, and got a five-cent raise. During the summers, I took the highest-paying manual labor jobs I could find. One summer, I worked for a utility company, using a jackhammer and digging ditches. Another summer, I worked for a publishing company, loading freight cars with seventy-pound bags of books and/or magazines, with the sun beating down on the roof and the sweat pouring off me. I actually enjoyed the hard manual labor, and after a hard, sweaty day, I often went home, showered, had a bite to eat and took Dad's car for a drive. Driving down the Outer Drive with the windows open and a cool breeze coming in was fantastic. No car air conditioning in those days.

I finished my last classes in June, 1950 and left campus. The graduation ceremony was a few weeks later, but I never returned for it. They mailed my diploma to me. I never asked my folks at the time, or later, what they thought of it, but as a parent myself, I have since wondered what they thought about this. So there I was, a college graduate, with no idea what I wanted to do. But I wasn't worried about it because I knew I could make a living.

Also, sometime during my first year or so at college, I read *Atlas Shrugged* by Ayn Rand (not an assigned reading) and thought to myself, "That's exactly how I feel and how I look at the world." Over the years, I read most of Ayn Rand's books, and a few years ago, I reread *Atlas Shrugged*. I still like her philosophy about the primacy and freedom of the individual and the idea that there is an objective reality. It fits well with my vision of freedom and responsibility.

I believe that our views are fashioned to a large extent by our experiences. My college experience was a bit unusual, since I finished in just three-and-a-half years, but it was not so unusual, at least then, that I chose to go to the in-state university, which was a lower-cost alternative. And it was somewhat unusual that I worked while going to school and during the summer vacations. Also, back then, we were focused on learning. There were no demonstrations on campus, no banning of speakers. I don't remember a single instance when a professor expressed his own political views in the classroom.

So, frankly, I don't understand and I am not sympathetic to what is going on at some of our campuses today. My involvement with the Miller Center gives me a lot of opportunities to talk to students and professors. I know that most students and schools are still focused on learning and do not experience some of the disruptions we hear about. But it does happen on some campuses, and I don't understand why the administration allows it. Back then, we were pretty focused on learning something, graduating, and getting on with our careers. I don't remember ever seeing a demonstration on campus.

I also am not sympathetic to students who choose to go to schools they can't afford, who don't work to pay for their education, who run up a big-time debt and then don't repay that debt. Of course, college was much less expensive then, even in inflation-adjusted dollars. Most of us went to less expensive state schools or other schools nearby. Nobody I knew went to one of the prestigious high-profile schools. Yet, in spite of, or maybe because of that, many of us went on to become very successful. Again, people are free to do as they choose but they are also responsible for the consequences of their actions.

And so I had finished the first phase of my life, which, unbeknownst to me, and with no planning on my part nor any push from my parents, built a work habit foundation for what was to come next. I had learned, and had come to believe in, self-reliance, the concept that "if it is to be, it is up to me." Benjamin Franklin and Abraham Lincoln, I later learned, were strong proponents of this belief. Also, this concept is a basis for realizing the promise in the Declaration of Independence that each of us is free to pursue our happiness and to improve our station in life through our own efforts.

And, fortunately for me, I grew up in an America that still valued those ideals, an America in which they could lead to great success.

15

MEANDERING
INTO A CAREER

So there I was, with a college degree, no money, and living at home. I can't remember being concerned about it. Howard, who had his degree in accounting and had easily passed the CPA exam, had started to work for his dad and was going to night school at Northwestern for an MBA degree. He helped with the accounts his dad had already, and then, whenever they picked up a new account, it became Howard's. It was a great way to start an accounting firm, which Howard built into a very successful practice in the years ahead with one hundred employees.

With nothing else to do, I also went to work for my dad in the chicken store, scraping the droppings off the pans and killing and dressing (plucking the feathers off) the chickens. This was not a career move, but I was able to make a little money while I figured out what to do next. I recommend that recent college graduates get into the labor market right away, even if it's at a level that is not commensurate with their education. It brings you down to earth in a hurry and teaches you the value and dignity of working. And, by the way, this and my other jobs during school always kept me connected to and sympathetic with average working people, no matter how much money I made. I guess this experience has made me unsympathetic to college graduates who go jobless and complain because they can't immediately find a job suitable for their educational background.

Anyhow, as I was thinking about what to do next, somehow—and I have no idea why—the thought of becoming a lumberjack popped into my head, and I thought, "Why not?" I saw an ad from a car dealer called "Z" Frank Chevrolet who was looking for someone to drive a car from Chicago to Portland, Oregon. Funny the way things work out: the dealer's son now belongs to the same country club I do. Anyhow, I applied for the job and was hired. They gave me a date when the car had to be delivered but did not specify the route, and that was their mistake.

It's about two thousand miles from Chicago to Portland, driving due west. But with the amount of time they gave me to make the trip, I figured I could see more of the country than that. After all, I had never travelled anywhere before, except to Champaign and to a few resort areas nearby, in Michigan and Wisconsin, so I decided to take the old, and then-famous, Route 66 from Chicago to Los Angeles and then take Highway One up the West Coast to Portland, a trip of almost three thousand miles. I was paying for the gas, so I thought it wouldn't make much difference to them.

And what a trip it was, down to St. Louis, through Missouri, the Ozarks, Oklahoma, New Mexico, Arizona, California, and then up to Portland. Seeing the Grand Canyon was quite an experience. To today's kids, some of whom study abroad and back-pack through Europe or fly to Asia or Israel without a second thought, it might not seem like much. But to me, back then, it was a real adventure.

On the way, I picked up a couple of hitchhikers, a young husband and wife, who rode with me for several days. I still remember what the husband said when I dropped them off. "Why did you pick us up?" he asked. "We could have been murderers." That had never occurred to me. Back then we didn't have nonstop cable TV news channels, twenty-four hours a day, turning a one-time incident into a virtual crime epidemic like they do today, so that everyone is afraid of everything.

In any event, by the time I got to Portland, just barely in time, I decided that I didn't want to be a lumberjack. So I stayed there a day or two and then took a train back to Chicago, giving me another opportunity to see more of the country. We have a pretty big country out West, which I still marvel at as I fly over it.

Back in Chicago, I still had no idea what I wanted to do. I took a job selling advertising for a small suburban paper in Park Ridge and I was doing okay, but when I found that the owner was lying about his circulation figures, I quit. I can't stand dishonesty. So I was out of work. My brother, Arnold, who had opened up a cut-up chicken store, needed some help and offered me a job. He and Dad had come up with a plan to start a chain of cut-up chicken stores, but that never worked out. I guess the women just preferred picking up their chicken at the supermarkets along with their other groceries.

One day, while I was mopping the floor, Uncle Dave, Mom's brother, stopped at the store and when he saw me mopping, he said, "What kind of a job is that for a college graduate? Why don't you come to work for me?" Dave, who had never gone to college, was a successful businessman. For some reason, he was always in awe of anyone with a college degree.

Universal Foods was a small but very well-run and very profitable manufacturer of soup concentrates and gelatin desserts for the restaurant and food-service industries. They were the number-two brand (Soup's On) in the field, always chasing the leader, but never catching up to it. What kept them in the game was that they would package private-label product, even in small quantities, so that different dealers in the same area could compete against one another.

I think it was this exposure to private label that eventually led me to focus on private labeling the products we sold at Quill—another example of a seemingly inconsequential experience that led me to a very important ingredient in our later success. At Quill, we did so much private labeling that eventually a study showed that our Quill brand was the fifth most recognized brand in the office products field, behind Scotch Tape, Swingline, and a few others.

Another thing that kept Universal in the game was their fantastic customer service. Uncle Dave may not have been the world's most aggressive marketer, but he ran a very good business with customer service at the top of the agenda and careful follow-up right behind that. To give great customer service to private-label customers, they would go through the extra cost of manufacturing and inventorying the unlabeled merchandise and then, when the orders came in, they would unpack the unlabeled jars, label them, and then repack them so they could be shipped within a day. That's another lesson I learned that helped us make Quill so successful years later.

Uncle Dave hired me to become a salesman. They had one salesman covering the country and they also exhibited at conventions. My training consisted of going along with this salesman on a few one-week trips; I then spent a month or so with a few of our distributors in the Chicago area, working with their salesmen, calling on restaurants, hospitals, schools, and other food-service facilities. Although it was a relatively short indoctrination period, it was evidently enough, because when I went out onto the road, I seemed to be prepared.

I bought a car, a Chevrolet, and since Dave and I were about the same size, he gave me a couple of his suits, which fit well, with minor alterations. They assigned me a territory from the Mississippi River to the Atlantic Ocean and from Canada to Florida, but I also remember making calls in Texas. I don't remember what my salary was to start, but I remember that five years later it was $115 per week, which would be about $1,000 per month today, adjusted for inflation, or $52,000 per year. I guess that's pretty comparable to what many young people are getting these days just out of college, although that was after five years on the job, so it was pretty low. Of course I spent most of those five years on the road on an expense account, and when I was home, I lived with my parents. So I saved a good bit of what I made.

Those five years turned out to be an invaluable educational experience, an MBA on steroids. I have come to believe that the smartest thing a young person could do is to get a great liberal arts education studying history, philosophy, and literature—with a few business classes, particularly economics, thrown in—and then either go to grad school and enter a profession such as accounting, engineering, law, architecture, etc., or go to work and learn all you need to know about business that way.

For five years, I spent most of my time on the road, working in small towns and midsize and larger cities. I learned and sharpened my selling skills and my ability to absorb rejection and move on, something that was essential when I started my own business and did a lot of cold canvassing. I also got a real bird's-eye view of how the distribution system in our country worked and how different business people ran their businesses. Very importantly, I was basically on my own: I created my own schedules and worked without supervision, which suited me just fine. It also prepared me for starting my own business.

I had the opportunity to work with hundreds of different food brokers and distributors and I could see and learn how they differed—and what made some so successful and why others were just hanging on. It was a great opportunity to study all these different entrepreneurs and to see how well our free-market system worked.

I saw some businessmen nimbly taking advantage of new opportunities, such as the then-new phenomenon of frozen foods, and saw others working hard to expand sales within their own product areas. Most salesmen worked hard to get orders, sometimes on price and other times on service, or just by establishing better relationships with the buyers.

But I learned that nothing ever happened until someone sold something. And all of this, all across the country, was taking place without government interference, so far as I knew. Everyone was just pursuing their own self-interest, and somehow it all worked. Everything came together and seemed to work well overall. Later, at a Miller Center Summer Institute, I learned that this was an example of Adam Smith's invisible hand theory at work. I guess this was an experience that pushed me toward wanting to get back to our basic free-market principles as envisioned by our Founders, when, years later, the government got more and more involved with business, and in our lives. At the time, I was learning first-hand how well and how efficiently the principles work.

With a very small sales force and a limited advertising budget, there was no way Universal Foods, or most smaller food manufacturers for that matter, could efficiently reach their distributors on their own. Universal had a network of food brokers across the country, each covering a specific local market area. They, in turn, called on wholesale grocers and others in their market area who could inventory and distribute our product to the users, which, in our case, were restaurants, schools, hospitals, and other food services operations. This was exactly the same kind of distribution system I later found in the office products industry, with large manufacturers having direct sales forces and smaller ones using brokers who handled a number of lines.

It was common for me to go into a market where the broker was selling our product to a few of the wholesale grocers in the area without ever calling on the coffee distributors, potato chip distributors, meat distributors, or other types of distributors that were selling to restaurants, hospitals, bars, and the like. I would go with the broker to call on his customers and pitch the Soup's On line. Sometimes I would hold sales meetings with their customer's sales force or even spend a few days working with a few of their salesmen to call on their customers, the users. Then I would always insist the brokers go beyond their usual customer base and call on the other types of distributors who could handle our product. It was amazing how much additional business we would pick up that way.

Working with the distributors' salesmen was another essential part of my education because, when I started Quill, that is exactly what I needed to do, sell to the user. Quill was basically a distributor, and everything I learned during those five years on the road became invaluable to me, much more so than anything I could have learned in a classroom. And it was a hell of an experience.

Here's an example. Working with a wholesale grocer's salesman, we might start at 8:30 a.m., make perhaps ten calls a day and often, at a hospital or very big restaurant, get an order for five cases of soup concentrate and fifteen cases of gelatin dessert. At the other end of the spectrum, working with a potato chip distributor, we would start at about 6:30 a.m. and make as many as one hundred calls a day, calling on bars and other fast-food type places, selling just a few boxes at a time, and ending the day in the early evening.

And there I was, just twenty-three, working with people who had decades of experience, pushing them to sell more of our product and, in some cases, pushing them to get out of their comfort zone and call on different types of distributors. I always wore a suit and tie and fedora, so I guess I looked the part, at least. What a fantastic learning experience it all was.

One lesson I learned, which I was able to observe just because of the times, was that if you are smart enough, you can turn potentially catastrophic changes into major advantages. For example, during that period when I was on the road, frozen food products were just coming into vogue. At the same time, ice distributors were becoming obsolete and going out of business as refrigeration and freezers were becoming common. But the smarter, more aggressive ice distributors realized that their heavily insulated warehouses were ideal for storing the new frozen food products, and they had sales forces and office operations and customers already in place. So they, the smarter ones, began distributing frozen foods instead of ice, and instead of going out of business, they grew quite a bit.

These new frozen food distributors also became new opportunities for us, and I made sure that every broker I worked with called on them. Most importantly, they taught me a great lesson about how you turn problems into opportunities, a lesson that has stayed with me all my life. To me, luck, most often, is just being prepared and then taking advantage of opportunities that come along. Even Dad got lucky when competition forced him to close the money-losing stores and focus on his few wholesale accounts. With the knowledge he gained from years of selling with the Metropolitan Life Insurance Company and with his own natural ability, he turned those few accounts into a very nice, comfortable living.

During my years on the road, in addition to the work, I had the opportunity to see the country. I would usually work in a town or city for one to several days and then spend several hours in the evening driving to the next town or city. I stayed in motels for seven dollars or so per night or in hotels for not much more. I spent many an evening reading in my hotel room or going to a movie. I remember a weekend when I ended up in the Smoky Mountains and decided to go horseback riding, and another weekend somewhere in the East, exploring caves and learning the difference between stalagmites and stalactites, those formations that grow from the floor or the ceiling of caves.

The stories about travelling salesmen and women may have some basis in fact, but I guess because I wasn't a drinker and didn't visit bars, I couldn't vouch for them. So almost all of my free time, most evenings and weekends, I spent reading, exploring the area, going to movies, and working out at the local YMCAs. Hotels and motels didn't have health clubs then. Looking back on it now, I suppose I could have somehow used my free time better. But since I was on the road most of the time and spent little time at home, I dated very seldom and certainly not seriously, until Audrey came into my life.

During my third year on the road, I was at home one day with my brother, Harvey, who was on leave from the Navy. He was talking on the phone to a girl he used to date in high school and he said, "Here, Jack, you ought to talk to Audrey," and handed me the phone. We talked for a while and hit it off pretty well, so I took her out. For the next six months or so, we would date when I was in town, which wasn't that often, or we would talk on the phone when I wasn't. Then, one day, she sent me a letter that went somewhat like this, "Jack, you are a nice guy and I am a pretty nice girl, and we seem to like one another, so maybe we ought to get married." I must have figured that she was right, so we got married. I was twenty-five and Audrey was twenty-two. That letter resurfaced again forty-five years later, after Aud had passed away, and I was dating Goldie, and we were looking through boxes of memorabilia for old pictures to display at my seventieth birthday party.

Aud's Dad, "Papa" Jerry, as our kids used to call him, offered us the option of a large wedding or a small wedding plus the difference in cash. Without hesitation, we opted for the small wedding and the difference, $5,000 ($65,000 in 2017) in cash.

Because we wanted Harvey at the wedding and his leave kept being pushed up, we had to push the wedding forward several times to, finally, October 25, 1954. I can only guess about why people thought we kept moving the wedding up. But we didn't have our first child, Judith, until three years later. Our marriage lasted for forty years before Aud died of lung cancer. And it was a fantastic marriage. Never an argument and always supportive. In many ways, primarily because of her tremendous, undemanding support, Aud deserves a good deal of credit for the success of Quill.

If there is anything I have learned about marriage, and I have had experience with two of them, plus listening to all my friends, it is that you don't just marry a person. You marry a family. And in my case, with Audrey, I hit the jackpot. My father-in-law, Jerry Weil, was in business with his brother Herb, and they had a sister, Viola. Jerry and my mother-in-law, Edna, and Audrey, an only child, lived in a small two-bedroom apartment on the second floor at 1200 West Addison, which was just one block west of Wrigley Field, home of the Cubs. Uncle Herb and Aunt Viola lived just around the corner, on Magnolia, in a two-flat, two-story apartment building that Uncle Herb owned. They lived with their parents on the first floor and Viola lived with her husband and their son, Don, also an only child, on the second floor.

Their parents had come over from Germany in the late 1800s and their father, Nathan, started out making a living by selling vegetables from a horse-drawn cart in the alleys before he opened a small grocery store on Broadway near Addison. I know from an old picture I saw that selling off a cart is what he did in Germany before they came to America.

When their father had a heart attack at the age of fifty, and the doctors told him he should no longer work, Jerry and Herb took over the grocery store. They made a success of it, not only by selling groceries from the store, but also by providing them to yacht owners in nearby Belmont Harbor and providing delivery service to condominium owners along Lake Shore Drive. Not a big business, but a comfortable living. Aud was brought up in a household where working long hours and being thrifty was the norm.

On the other hand, my Dad, while working at the Metropolitan, had the attitude that "there was more where that came from," possibly because his good-paying job had protected him from the Depression. The Weils, on the other hand, always lived with the Depression-induced fear that there might not always be more. They lived very conservatively, yet were reasonably comfortable. They certainly were not stingy, but they were prudent. For me they were a wonderful model of self-sufficiency, hard work, and prudence. Between my folks and Audrey's, we had a wonderful support system with plenty of room to plot our own course.

A few months before we got married, Audrey and I bought a home that was under construction in Highland Park. It was on Ridge Road, an unpaved gravel street, and it was one of hundreds of almost identical homes that were being put up in that subdivision. It was a small split-level with a half-basement and crawl space, three bedrooms, two baths, living room, and kitchen on a decent-sized lot. The price was $19,600 (about $250,000 in 2017). There was no garage and, in fact, no driveway. We would drive out on weekends to see the progress but didn't want to be there during the week to make any suggestions. We couldn't afford any extras.

Unlike what's going on today, the custom then was to put twenty-five percent down and get a mortgage for the rest. So we put down $5,000 and had a $14,600 mortgage, so our monthly payments were $99 for the mortgage and $16 for taxes, or $115 total, which was exactly one week's pay.

The house wasn't ready until a few months after we were married. When we moved in, I spent every weekend that first summer digging out a driveway by hand and hauling the dirt around the corner in a wheelbarrow to dump in an empty lot. I enjoyed the work, but it was a dumb thing to do. As tight as money was, I should have had the builder or someone with the right equipment do it in a single day.

Our folks bought us a refrigerator, stove, and dishwasher, and Aud's grandparents bought us some lawn furniture that became our living room furniture for the next six years until we could afford regular furniture. Aud didn't complain at all. She found an office job a few miles away so she could walk to work, since I needed the car. About five or six years later I bought her a very nice used Ford coupé for about $250, and she was thrilled with it.

For a year after we were married, I continued to travel, but I cut my trips down to one or two weeks at a time. I also took over the advertising from Uncle

Dave, which he was happy to give up. So that gave me some more time to stay in town, working in the office. However, I was still traveling more than a happily married man should, so I decided to leave Universal Foods and take a job where I would be home all the time. And this began another stage of my working MBA program.

While working at Universal, we needed some custom-made cases to carry samples in a professional manner. I had found a company, the Knickerbocker Case Company, that manufactured such cases and also sold regular briefcases made by other manufacturers. In the process of designing and ordering the cases, I got to know the new owner of the company, and he asked if I would help him design a new catalog, featuring the custom capabilities and the standard briefcases they distributed.

I don't remember how he decided to ask me to do that because I had no experience with mail order. However, it was something I could do at night and on weekends, even when I was on the road, without taking me away from my regular job, so I agreed to do it.

When I decided to leave Universal, I struck a deal with the owner of Knickerbocker, and I became the president of the new division of the company that sold the standard briefcases made by other manufacturers, which we included as part of our offering. I was in charge of mail order and also of direct selling to large companies in Chicago that had big sales forces. My salary remained at $115, but I would own twenty-five percent of the new division and I would pay for it out of profits.

However, after one year, the owner decided to sell the company and move to California. I didn't like the people he sold to and decided not to stay. Although my division had made a profit that first year, I didn't get any of it. But he did tear up my non-compete agreement, which became very important to me.

So, there I was, married, with a home and mortgage—and without a job. I tried finding some sales jobs but I was asking for $10,000 per year ($130,000 in 2017), which some evidently felt was too much. At one place, I took, and evidently flunked, a psychological test. They were probably right, because I think I would have made a difficult employee, not being in charge. I had been working pretty much independently since leaving college and had been very independent for many years before that.

In any event, it didn't take me long to decide that what I really wanted to do was to go into business for myself. But what business? The only thing I could think of was that I had a few customers in Chicago who bought briefcases from me. I knew I couldn't live on that alone. But what else did they buy? Well, they were businesses, so I knew they bought office supplies. So, with no further research, I decided to go into the office supply business. I visited a few office supply stores and, fortunately for me, found I couldn't afford to buy even the smallest of them. The boredom of running a retail store would have killed me.

So I found a wholesaler who was relatively new to the wholesaling end of the business, and who would bend the rules a bit to sell to me if I put up a $300 deposit (about $2,700 today). I asked my father-in-law if he would lend me $2,000 ($26,000 today), which he agreed to do. My dad let me put a phone in his live poultry store and agreed to answer any calls for me while I was out selling. The wholesaler supplied me with some catalogs that I rubberstamped with the name of the new company, Quill Office Supply Company. I had business cards printed and I was in business.

By the way, most people who know me thought that I decided on the name Quill because of Dad's chicken store. But actually, when I decided to go into the business, Aud and I visited Howard Bernstein's house one evening, and we sat around trying to figure out a name. One of us came up with the idea that, since the Declaration of Independence was signed by a quill pen—why not call the company Quill? Forty-three years later, Quill was known nationwide for low prices and fantastic service and, as I have mentioned, a survey showed that Quill was one of the top five office products brands recognized in the United States. I guess a name is what you make of it. And a life is what you make of it. As our Declaration promised, I was in my own Pursuit of Happiness.

16

BUILDING A BUSINESS THROUGH HARD WORK AND SWEAT EQUITY

Contrary to everything they teach, I did no research when I decided to go into the office supply business—not a smart move. I had no idea how big the field was or what the competition was like. Early on, someone at the wholesaler asked me, "Why do you want to be in the office supply business? There are over 150 dealers in Chicago already."

As I remember, that didn't faze me at all. I just figured that I could go out there and get enough business to make a living. I had been competing against others in the food business, so what else was new? Also, fortunately for me, I had picked a field that was quite large, although it didn't look like it, because most of the dealers were small retailers, and I could grow my business without having to take over a big portion of the market. Today the biggest dealers are doing in the tens of billions of dollars in volume.

As for a mission and a business plan, I didn't have a formal, well-thought-out strategy. I guess my mission in the beginning was to make a living and my strategic plan was to do it by selling at discounted prices and to give the best service possible, better than anyone else. And that mission, to offer great customer service at low prices, continued to be Quill's central mission. It's also the mission of Millbrook Real Estate, our new family business, now tweaked to read, fanatical tenant service.

As for a business plan, it was simply that I would go out every day calling on businesses, trying to sell office supplies. Then, if I sold anything, at 7:30 the next morning I would call into the wholesaler to order the items I had sold the day before. Then I would start calling on more potential customers—cold calling, just knocking on doors. At about three in the afternoon, I would pick up whatever I had ordered from the wholesaler, rush back to Dad's chicken store, sort and wrap the merchandise and rush it to the UPS terminal at the intersection of Lawrence and Western Avenues to make the last truck by 6:30, so it could be delivered the next day.

So, if someone ordered something on a Monday, they would have it by Wednesday. Back then, that was pretty good service. Forty-three years later, if someone ordered by 6:30 at night, they would have their order the next day, anywhere in the country. We had nine well-stocked distribution centers by then, so we could provide next-day delivery anywhere in the country. We had improved and so had the delivery services. These days, even same-day service is possible in some areas.

Believe it or not, back then, most dealers were selling at full list price, so when we began advertising discount prices, other dealers started to call us "that dirty price cutter." Some others sold at discount prices, but they never advertised them. We did. When Harvey joined me a year and a half after I started, it began to get confusing, because it became harder and harder to keep track of the prices we had used to sell—to various customers—on the thousands of different products the wholesalers showed in their catalogs. So we decided to classify customers by potential volume and then give either 10, 15 or 20 percent off on every item regardless of the discounts we received when we bought the different items. And, much later, we came out with our own catalogs, and we advertised net discounted pricing based on our cost and on the competition, with four columns of further quantity discounts. The prices applied to everyone. This kept things simple and allowed us to eventually create our own call center, with hundreds of customer service people taking orders.

In any event, back in the beginning, after I dropped off the packages at the UPS terminal, I drove home, arriving by about 7:30. Later that evening, Aud would type up the invoices while I would do other office work. Once she complained that she couldn't get something else done because there were seven invoices to type up. The business had begun to grow. (When we sold the business, we were probably shipping in the neighborhood of thirty thousand orders a day, with UPS dropping off and picking up trailers at our docks all day long.)

My first month I sold $960 worth of merchandise (a little over $12,000 in 2017) and, after gas, phone bills, shipping, etc., I had a profit of around $30

($390 today). And we made a profit every month after that. For six months I didn't take any money out of the business, living on our savings and on Aud's salary. I would start out the week with about $25 in my pocket and by Friday, after paying for gas and lunches (usually a hamburger at McDonald's), end up with less than a dollar.

About six months after I started, Aud became pregnant and soon had to leave her job. By then I was able to draw enough to pay the bills, thank goodness. As we paid our personal bills, I would write a check from the business to ourselves for enough to cover the checks we had written.

My friend Howard, of course, became our accountant. He had given me my first order, for about $9.60 ($120 today). Howard remained our accountant until he sold his accounting firm and went into the mergers and acquisitions business. When we sold Quill to Staples in 1998, he managed the transaction for us and helped get us a very good deal. That was a fun sight. I remember a meeting in the kitchen of my home with four or five Goldman Sachs people, my brothers Harvey and Arnold, myself, and Howard. One of the Goldman Sachs people was always on the phone, another was crunching numbers, and the others were talking with Howard and us.

Howard wasn't just a great accountant. He also gave us great advice, such as "Have a profit-sharing, not a pension, plan." And, when we bought our first building, "Own it personally, not through the business." That last piece of advice actually launched us, years later, into the real estate business. Until our brother Arnold, who also was a CPA, joined us twenty-five years after we started, Howard was our main financial advisor as well as our accountant.

After he got out of the Navy, Harvey went to work for an electric supply company near the wholesaler I was using. I would stop there every Thursday to chat a bit with him and soon started to suggest that he come into the business with me. He gave it some thought and soon decided to do it. He borrowed money from his mother-in-law to invest in the business and we became partners.

The first thing we needed to do was to get a place where we could set up an office. We couldn't keep operating out of Dad's store; he didn't have room for the two of us. Also, I couldn't keep using the extra bedroom in my home as our office. Harvey and I needed an office where we could meet and work. Audrey's Uncle Herb came to the rescue. In his two-flat he had a coal bin in the basement that he wasn't using since they had converted to gas a few years earlier. The only problem was that there was about a ton of coal still in it.

Harvey and I rented a truck and spent a whole weekend shoveling up coal out of the coal bin into a wheelbarrow and then into the truck parked in the alley. After the truck was filled, we drove it to a landfill and unloaded it—and so on, until the coal bin was empty. We then hosed down the bin until it was clean, and painted it with paint that was left over from painting our children's rooms. Since I had a girl and he had a boy, our décor was blue and pink. We used a couple of old enamel kitchen tables for desks, put in phones that were also connected to Dad's store a couple of blocks away, and we were good to go.

We hired our first employee to do billing and other bookkeeping part-time while we were in Uncle Herb's basement. She often had to duck between drying laundry to get into the office. Over the next year or two, we began to take over more and more of the basement as we started to inventory some items. By the way, we paid Uncle Herb exactly what we had been paying Dad—nothing. We were very grateful to Uncle Herb, as we had been to Dad.

Again, opting for simplicity, we divided the city in half, with Harvey taking everything north of downtown and me taking the downtown area and every-thing south. Also, we each took a salary of $115 a week, net after taxes. Initially, we weren't making enough to cover both salaries, but with both of us out selling, we were soon able to cover them.

Right after I started the business, before Harvey joined me, I sent out 150 penny-postal cards (yes, they cost just one cent, including the postage) to com-panies I had called on, listing five items for sale. I got a few responses, and a month or so later followed that up with a one-page, one-sided, eight-and-a-half by eleven-inch flyer with more sale items listed. Over the next few years, that was followed by more and larger mailings.

A few years later we moved to a small storefront location. Because we didn't want people looking in or coming in off the street, we painted over the windows. We were using the store as both an office and warehouse. By then we had two employees, one to do the billing and bookkeeping and to be a back-up on the phones, and the other to primarily handle the phones, receive merchandise, etc. By then our sales flyers kept growing—to eight pages, sixteen pages, thirty-two pages, and more.

One day, when we met in the office at 7:30 a.m., as usual, the phones became so busy that neither of us was able to get out to sell. When this began to happen more frequently, we decided that we would only go out if someone wanted to give us a big furniture order and needed some help. Without planning to, we had slid into the mail-order business.

This gradual growth—with a slow evolution and showing a profit each month—was in stark contrast to some of today's start-ups, where they raise a lot of venture capital and go for growth regardless of profits (or losses). But I suspect that most start-ups today still follow the old-fashioned way, regardless of the idea you get from the press about the high-tech start-ups. It's more boring, but it still works.

In any event, our mailings increased in both the size of the flyers and the number of people we were mailing to. It wasn't long before we outgrew the store. By then, Dad had decided to close his live poultry business so he could handle just his few wholesale accounts who used chicken-meat in the manufacture of their products, frozen pizza, chicken-soup base, and so on. So all he needed was a desk and a phone. We converted his store into offices, and his large, garage-like structure, where they used to keep the live chickens, became our warehouse. Our roles had changed. We were now answering his phones when he was out making sales calls. We also paid him rent, which was a nice extra source of money for him. By then we had seven employees.

During that time, we decided we could make more money if we channeled more sales into the expanding number of products we bought directly from the manufacturers and inventoried, eliminating the wholesaler's markup. The way to do this, we felt, was to come out with our own full-line catalog and pick even more products to inventory. But that would take more money than we had, so we decided to borrow from a bank—for the first *and last* time in what turned out to be our forty-three years in business.

Adjacent to Dad's building was a vitamin bottling and distribution business. They needed more space, so they moved out. We assumed their lease and broke through the walls to connect the two buildings. I took over a small office in that building and, with Carole Anderson, one of our employees, locked myself in there to work on creating the catalog. I began rough page layouts and wrote all the copy myself. I found a good art agency to turn the rough draft into a really nice-looking hundred-page catalog.

Meanwhile, we were inventorying more and more lines, filling up the new space. Within a year, after a lot of hard work, the catalog was ready to be mailed. We hired two more people to help handle the additional volume that we expected to be coming in and we mailed out the catalogs. Then we waited—and waited.

After a few months, when we didn't see the big increase in business that we had expected, we had to lay off one of the extra people we had hired. That was the last time we ever hired in anticipation of projected sales and the last time we ever laid off anyone for lack of business. Lesson learned. In the meantime, our agreement with the bank required us to pay back a certain amount on the loan every three months. As tough as it was to do without the big expected increase in volume, we somehow managed to meet that commitment.

One day, when I went to the bank to make a payment and renew the reduced note, a new young loan officer (they kept changing) said to me, "Why don't you pay this loan off like you're supposed to?" I said, "Damn it, we are paying it off as we agreed to." Two days later, we switched to a new bank, American

National, and we stayed with them for the next thirty-five years until we sold the company. Of course, they never made a lot of money on us, because we never again borrowed money, growing strictly on our own reinvested cash.

Then we made a bad mistake. Because the catalog wasn't attracting the business we projected—so much for projections—we decided not to mail another catalog and I began to cannibalize the catalog artwork to use in our flyers. A few years later, when we decided once again to come out with our own full-line catalog, we had to start from scratch again with new artwork.

Fortunately, at the same time, we made a good decision. Because we were struggling, we needed to decide what to do going forward. One evening we met with Dad and my father-in-law, Jerry, to talk about it. There was talk about abandoning mail order and going out on the street again, selling. I adamantly refused to do that, so the upshot was that we tightened our belts and stayed with the mail-order model.

It wasn't too long before our volume grew to easily cover all the added expenses and, in fact, we soon needed to move to even larger quarters. We found a really nice building for sale, with twenty-seven thousand square feet of space and two recessed loading docks just a few blocks away, on Belmont near Clark Street. Harvey, Dad, and I managed to put together enough money for the down payment, and we bought it. By then our volume and profits could easily cover the monthly mortgage payments. This was a pattern we followed in our later expansions: not taking on added expenses until we could easily afford them. Dad rented his place out to someone else and he now had rental income from two buildings, plus his wholesale chicken business.

Things were finally looking up for Dad. Mom and Dad had moved to a very nice building on Lake Shore Drive with a beautiful view of the lake, and we even talked Dad into buying a Cadillac. He was so proud to drive that! It had been a long, difficult struggle, but Dad was finally doing better than when he was at Metropolitan, plus he was in control of his own life to boot. When we built out our office space in our new place, Dad had a handsome wood-paneled office and all the secretarial help he needed, which wasn't much, because he was a bit worn down by the years of hard work that he had been through and he didn't feel like struggling anymore to build his business larger. He was content. So he would spend the mornings working on his business and then spend some part of the afternoons working on our customer mailing lists. He took great pleasure in seeing how big it was growing.

As I mentioned, Howard's advice was to buy the building in our own names, not as part of the business. That was great advice, because that launched us into eventually owning nine distribution centers around the country plus a huge corporate headquarters with a lot of extra land around it. And when we sold the business, the deal was structured so that we had to sell the real estate along with it (except for the empty land around our headquarters) and we made a nice profit on that. Also, that eventually launched us into becoming real estate developers and investors after we sold Quill. Again, it's interesting how one thing leads to the next, and how it can all be good if you make the right decisions and work hard at it. As I am endlessly telling my grandchildren, "Actions have consequences, and we are all responsible for our own actions."

At about this time, when we moved into the building on Belmont with over thirty employees, our profits were growing nicely and we wanted to share some of the growth of the company with them. We began looking at pension plans (guaranteed benefits) and profit sharing (guaranteed contribution) plans. When we asked a pension plan expert how much we would need to contribute each year to the plan to fund it for the promised benefits, he asked, "How much do you want to contribute?" He explained that we didn't have to fully fund it. With Howard's counsel, we immediately opted for a profit-sharing plan, where you decide what percentage of your profits you want to contribute and then, at the end of the year, you write a check for that amount that goes into a separate fund not connected to your business.

One employee, Wally Wenzel, started with us when we took over Dad's old store. He stayed with us, working in the warehouse, until many years later, when he retired with over a million dollars in his profit-sharing account. In the meantime, every day we read about burdensome, underfunded pension plans. With a profit-sharing plan, there are no unfunded liabilities, which was always a basic rule for us. It's a shame our governments don't follow the same ethical and practical concept, instead of using underfunded pension plans, which are now bankrupting states.

During this time, I also managed to work out almost every day with a full set of weights in my basement, often rising at 5:00 a.m. to manage a workout. I also did short stints of Judo, Aikido, and Karate, but didn't really get too enthused about them. However, handball did become a passion of mine and I played that for about thirty-five years, twice a week. Many of our friends over the years were fellow handball players.

In the meantime, after seventeen years of living in Highland Park, we sold the house for $35,000 (over $206,000 in 2017) and moved to Lincolnwood, a suburb right next to Chicago, which was a short commute to the office. Aud had wanted to move for a few years, but I was reluctant, until I was involved in an accident on the highway on my way home one night. A telephone company van veered into me, rolled over on its back, and forced me into a guardrail.

Fortunately, I wasn't injured, but I finally decided that the long commute was crazy. In addition, Audrey was always concerned that the house, which still stands today, wasn't built as well as it should have been and that it would collapse one day. So we bought a really solid, much nicer house in 1971 for $75,000 (over $440,000 in 2017).

So, in the year I was turning forty years old, I suddenly had a much larger mortgage and although I could well afford it by then, for some reason it almost drove me into a depression—so much so that one day my dad said, "Jack, get over it. Do something to the house to make it your own." After several months, I did get over it: I enjoyed the short commute to work and being just five minutes from where I played handball. Aud loved it. I remember one time she told me how she was working in the kitchen, cooking and baking, and the sun was coming in, and she thought to herself, "I hope no one comes in and stops me." Life was good.

Both of our girls, Judith and Sheri (although then she was known as Sharon), went through the Lincolnwood school system and to Niles West, a really good high school. Judith became a fine gymnast and competed successfully throughout her high school career. I made sure to take time off from work to attend her meets, one of the very few things for which I would take time off. Somewhere I have all of her events on film.

Other than those activities, most of the time my life consisted of work, leaving home at seven in the morning, and not getting back until seven or so in the evening. We always tried to have dinners together, but if I had to work late, Aud always had a warm dinner waiting for me. However, if I was late getting home because I stopped off to play handball, I had cold leftovers. I also often brought some work home and we went to the office half-days on Saturdays.

The business continued to grow and we soon had about forty employees at the Belmont location, a virtual United Nations, with people from a variety of countries. Harvey handled the reordering and everyday operations while I managed the advertising, merchandising, and the purchasing of new lines and items. Soon we were again running out of space and needed to expand.

We found a piece of land where we could build a new facility. Dad and I planned to see our banker to set up the finances for the deal. On the way, we stopped to have lunch with Aud and Mom, who was still working downtown. Then we stopped at a tailor where I was having a new suit made. In those days we always went to work in a suit and tie.

It was February, 1970. As I was trying on the suit, Dad went to a desk to call the office. On the way back, he said, "I feel dizzy," and with that he fell to the floor. I became frantic. Someone called the Fire Department. Someone else asked if he had medicine and we searched his pockets and found nitro pills, which we put under his tongue. In a minute or two, the fire ambulance arrived and they took Dad to the hospital. I anxiously waited outside the room where they had taken Dad, very upset. When they came out and told me that Dad was dead, I burst into tears.

I loved my dad. He had been a bit of a rebel in his youth, running away to join the Coast Guard at fourteen and then the Navy at sixteen. I guess that part of him was why he let me be my own boss and live my life my way—so long as I was honest and had good values. He taught me to drive when I was about twelve and let me drive the family to Wisconsin, as he sat next to me, when I was thirteen. I got my driver's license the day I turned fifteen.

During the thirteen years from the time I started the business up until Dad died, we saw each other almost every day. I don't remember us ever having an argument. His death was a real blow. But at least he had achieved some success in the final few years, and had the *nachas* (pleasure and happiness) of seeing his sons solidly on the road to success.

When they came out and told me that Dad was dead, I immediately called Harvey so he could meet me at the store where Mom was working. That way we could both tell her what had happened. We went to her department and talked to her supervisor, who had us stay in her office until she got Mom. When Mom came into the office and saw both of us, she immediately knew something bad had happened to Dad. She burst into tears. Later, after the funeral and the Shiva, we asked Mom to come to work for us so she would be near us every day. She had no office skills, but she was a really hard worker and she found her spot in the mailroom, where she continued to work until her death eighteen years later.

We lost interest in moving, and stayed on Belmont Avenue for another few years until we absolutely had to move. We found a really good broker who came up with a good piece of land in Northbrook, not far from where I used to live in Highland Park. So now I would need to commute again, except in the opposite direction. He also came up with a clever, perfectly legal way of doing a three-way deal where we could avoid paying capital gains tax on the sale of our building. As Justice Learned Hand famously wrote back in 1934, in *Helvering v. Gregory* (69 F.2d 809 (2d Cir. 1934), 810), "Any one may so arrange his affairs that his taxes shall be as low as possible; he is not bound to choose that pattern which will best pay the Treasury; there is not even a patriotic duty to increase one's taxes."

Or, as Howard often says, "It's your patriotic duty to keep money out of the hands of the government."

We purchased the land and began designing and building the new facility. During the building process, Harvey spent full-time on the project and I ran the business. At the same time, he found a piece of land near the new facility and bought it to build a new home for his family. Using just half the land we had for the building, we reserved the other half for expansion. We built a very nice building, with good warehouse space and four loading docks and very nice offices that became our home-base for the next seven years.

Shortly after that, when Harvey and Jan were vacationing in California, they visited with our brother, Arnold, who was divorced and was living alone. Harvey asked Arnold, who was a CPA, to come to Chicago and join the company. After seeing our financials and giving it some thought, he joined us and took over the accounting, billing, and accounts receivable functions. (How proud and happy Dad would have been to see his three sons working together in the business.) Arnold soon also took over human resources, but only after we met with the management consultant we hired to help us.

That was some session for the three Miller brothers! We had been having a few issues among ourselves, so we called in this individual to help us work through them. The discussion became very intense and I began to hyperventilate or something. They called an ambulance, thinking I was having a heart attack. Thankfully, it was a false alarm.

As a result of that meeting with the consultant, we made clearly defined divisions of responsibilities within the company, with each of us having total authority in our own areas. We followed this new management approach for the next twenty-five years until we sold the company. Working with my brothers turned out to be not only great for the business but also a great personal experience. Once we sorted out our responsibilities, we worked together terrifically and the business thrived. Any disagreements concerned only the best ways to grow the business, and never personal issues.

Of course, our offices were next to one another, and we had lunch together almost every day. So, we were always up-to-date on what was going on in all areas and could voice our opinions. It really worked beautifully.

The business continued to grow and prosper. We kept growing at a nice clip, often at double-digits each year. This was in the 1970s, and things were going nicely. In those days we were so busy running the business that we spent little time reading and thinking about the news. All of our money was tied up in the business, which was growing steadily, so when the stock market went down by as much as forty percent or so, it didn't mean much to us. But then the Federal Reserve began lowering interest rates to encourage growth and employment, and the Nixon Administration put on wage and price controls in the early

1970s—and then took them off. That forced people to try to catch up, which led to tremendous inflation.

And, of course, the government never learned from that experience, and over the years it has been increasingly interfering with the marketplace. Right now, as I am writing this, the government has pushed interest rates so low in their effort to restart a sluggish economy, that people can't make enough interest on their bonds to pay all their bills—like a good friend of mine who worked hard his whole life, paid off his mortgage, paid fully for his kid's college education and put away money for his retirement. He is afraid to gamble in the stock market, so it's all in low-interest bonds, and he has to eat into the principal and pray that he has enough to see himself and his wife through to the end of their lives. In the meantime, I am able to borrow at very low rates to buy more commercial real estate. It's not right. It's not fair. It's not what our Founders intended.

As a result of that inflation in the 1970s, our vendors began raising prices every few months, in some cases not even bothering to print new price lists, just using the old ones and rubber stamping them with some tagline like, add 5 percent or 10 percent to all prices. We were mailing our customers every three months, guaranteeing prices for six months, the life of our main-line catalog. But with these rapid-fire cost escalations, we couldn't continue to do so. We decided to mail our customers monthly, guaranteeing prices just for that month, whether the items were shown in the flyers or just in that year's catalog.

Again, some event over which we had no control changed things dramatically. The unintended consequence of those additional mailings was that our business exploded. Of course, I would later jokingly call it marketing genius. But the truth was that, when we were forced to mail our customers on a monthly instead of a quarterly basis, they bought more from us, ordering more often. Following the logic that if more was good, then even more would be better, we began pushing this rule to the limit over the following years, until we were mailing our customers five times a month and they began complaining. But at that time, in the late 1970s, when we started mailing them monthly, our business grew 90-plus percent each year for two years running.

Our warehouse crew became so overwhelmed that we fell behind in filling orders by almost a week, which caused even more work as customers started calling again to find out where their orders were. Harvey changed from a suit to jeans and took control of the warehouse, putting all the orders in a file cabinet, filed by date received. Then, methodically, with lots of overtime and additional help, we got caught up and back to our same-day shipment standard within a week or so.

A few years later, by the time we were able to focus on the consequences of this explosion in business for our physical plant, we were operating out of seven different buildings in the industrial park. We discovered that, even if we built on our vacant land, we couldn't expand our building enough to handle all the extra office and warehouse space we needed. So, we had to move again.

We had moved five times already. This time, I decided we needed to buy enough land so we would never need to move again. We hired a real estate agent, but after many months without results, I decided to try myself. Someone had mentioned to me that the gas company kept records of all the vacant land anywhere in the Chicagoland area, so I went there. In a room filled with files and maps I met an old man—at least, in those days he seemed old to me, but he would probably seem young to me now—who listened to me describe what I was looking for. He said he couldn't think of anything like that, and I left. The next day I got a call from him, and he said he had found something I might like, a twenty-seven-acre former tree nursery in Lincolnshire, just fifteen minutes further north from where we were.

When I went to see it, I immediately fell in love with it as I walked through the overgrown, neglected, and very serene tree nursery. We met with the Fiore brothers, whose recently deceased brother had owned the property, and we immediately agreed on a price. I asked for a few months' delay so we could give our broker an opportunity to find a better deal, if possible, which the Fiores verbally agreed to.

A few months later, when our broker couldn't find anything as good, much less better, we sat down with the Fiores and both of our lawyers to finalize the deal. When the lawyers started trying to renegotiate it, I stopped them, saying, "We have already agreed on the deal. You guys just put it down on paper." The Fiore brothers were old school gentlemen; with them a verbal agreement meant something. Lawyers often kill deals, and we didn't let that happen here.

That was back in 1982. By 1998, when we sold the business, we had doubled the size of the warehouse and tripled the size of the office, and we still had land left over. In fact, we bought another twenty-five acres adjacent to us just because it became available. We also had built and leased to the company nine additional distribution centers around the country. We were sort of sliding into the real estate business.

We had become one of the largest office products dealers in the country. And in the fall of 1982, I began writing a biannual State of the Industry report, a four-page newsletter on my views of the industry—what I felt was happening and would be happening—that I sent to all of our vendors. My observations were based on all the many conversations I had with the salespeople who visited us, on conversations with the owners and managers of our vendors and on some surveys I conducted, plus what I picked up from newspaper stories.

These reports soon began to be followed and even read by vendors at their sales meetings. When you talked with enough people in the industry and read enough in the industry journals and attended the conventions and really paid attention, it wasn't that tough to connect the dots and become pretty accurate on reporting what was happening and predicting what might happen.

I did this just because I enjoyed writing and I thought it would be fun to share what I had been learning. I kept it up for eleven years and many of my predictions came to pass. For example, starting in the late 1980s, I began reporting on the emerging office products supermarket phenomenon, which was just starting in our industry. I predicted that it would succeed and that it would change the industry.

That all started when Tom Stemberg, a great entrepreneur in Massachusetts, was frustrated one Sunday when he couldn't find a typewriter ribbon he needed to type up a job application. So, he decided that the office products industry needed superstores like those in the grocery business, where he came from. That was in 1985. In May of 1986, he opened the first Staples store, and today they do over $21 billion in volume, with stores and salesforces all over the country, and with a strong mail-order and online presence as a result of buying Quill in 1998. But, of course, just as it has happened throughout history—think of Montgomery Ward, Sears Roebuck, etc.—just as they revolutionized the industry, others (Amazon, etc.) have come along to do the same to them. Staples is now struggling to survive and, in fact, in 2017 they sold the company along with Quill, which, they tell me, was their most profitable division.

The office products industry had been highly fragmented, with over fifteen thousand dealers, mostly small and mostly retail and all selling at retail prices. Then, far fewer in number were the contract dealers with salespeople on the street and three good-sized mail-order dealers, of which we were one. Pretty soon after Staples started, others followed, until there were close to thirty superstores, but then the weaker ones dropped out until it dwindled down to just three and, as I said, it is now down to two, Staples and Office Depot, and they are under attack by the big-box and online operators, who offer much lower prices.

The free market is a great system. In the office products business, we saw how it created more value and improved service for the consumer. We saw it with the advent of the superstores, which drove prices down for the consumers, even the small retail customers. And now the superstores are being undersold by online retailers like Amazon who have a much more efficient business model. The consumer wins.

When we started, as I have said, we were the first mail-order dealer, the dirty price cutter who published discount prices. Before that, most dealers sold at the manufacturers' list prices. And then, when the superstores came on the scene, their prices were even lower, often much lower. As the superstores expanded, the inefficient dealers began to go out of business, unable to compete. Eventually, ten thousand of them were driven out while five thousand survived.

Because of our great service and our competitive prices, we were able to survive and even grow. But one of our mail-order competitors was driven out of business and the other continued to grow because of their fantastic service, and because they opened operations successfully in Europe, where the superstores had not yet started. As part of my Industry Report predictions, I began to say that these three superstores were here to stay. The industry, as most dealers had viewed it for years, was not small; it was actually very large. Most dealers were doing less than a million dollars, often just a few hundred thousand in volume. Some contract stationers, though not many, who were selling to large businesses at competitive prices, were doing as much as $20–30 million. Quill and one of our mail-order competitors had sales in the hundreds of millions of dollars, but the superstores were beginning to sell in the billions.

Even though we were already selling at discounted prices, we felt we had to match, or beat, the superstores' even lower prices. So, starting on February 1, 1990, we cut all our already discounted prices even more. From then until August or September of that same year, we didn't make any money. We went on a cost-cutting binge. We had been preparing all our employees for what was to come. We told them to find any savings they could, even if it meant the elimination of their own job. We promised that no one would be laid off and that, if some positions were eliminated, we would find other positions for them.

Everyone jumped in with ideas. The people doing the work always know where the waste is. One of the janitors even suggested changing to longer-lasting light bulbs in the Exit signs so, while they cost a bit more, we would save on the labor of changing them. No savings was too small, and some were significant. Of course, we also put pressure on our vendors to get better prices.

By September, we started making money again and we turned a profit for the full year. Afterwards, looking back on this, we kicked ourselves for not finding all these savings before we were forced to. We could have really improved our bottom line! A chapter in my book, *Simply Success*, is titled, "You Can, Too, Argue with Success!" (Miller 2008, 111–116)—and this experience showed how we could have done that. This also reinforced my belief in how much waste there had to be in most businesses and in government. I can't even imagine how great the savings could be.

So we met the superstore challenge. We continued to do well and continued to grow. But the next big challenge was the Y2K hysteria as we approached the year 2000. Everyone started going crazy, almost predicting the end of civilization as we knew it. They said that computer systems would malfunction, shutting down much of the world's infrastructure. The best brains in the country were predicting chaos unless computer systems were modified.

For the two years just before we sold to Staples in 1998, we spent in excess of $20 million redoing our systems, which hurt our bottom line. So, when we sold to them at a multiple of profits, we suffered for getting caught up in that hysteria, which, like so many crises, never happened. Almost no business computer systems were affected. Life went on. We had wasted a lot of money and effort just at the wrong time, right before the sale. Still, I guess it is hard to know which crises are legitimate.

But that wasn't the only mistake (or failure) that we had in our business careers. At one point we decided that we should expand into the higher-end office furniture business. So we bought a distributor who had a chain of about six furniture showroom/stores around the city, plus a few outside salesmen. This distributor was losing money. We had already been selling a lot of office furniture through our catalogs, but it was mostly lower-end or middle-range furniture, and we would sell one or two desks or file cabinets at a time. We were doing a lot of volume in office furniture, but none of it was in the higher-end lines, and none of it was where we did office layouts and installations. But we thought—and this is a mistake that lots of businessmen make—that because we were so successful at what we were doing that we could do almost anything. We were wrong. After a couple of costly and aggravating years, we simply closed that business down. We just didn't have, nor did we hire, the right kind of experience. A common but dumb mistake.

The other major mistake we made was different. Our chief mail-order competitor was enjoying so much success in Europe that we thought we would give it a try. But they were smarter than we were. They had expanded to Europe. We decided to open up in Canada. We were getting some incidental business from the Canadians, so we decided to open a warehouse in Canada and mail to businesses there. What we didn't realize was that Canada is a country that is a few miles deep (where most of the population was) and five thousand miles wide—a logistical nightmare. It is also a country that is divided by two languages, English and French. We opened a warehouse in Toronto, and Harvey's son, Steve, went there to run it. He did a good job, but we were unable to overcome the geographic and language barriers, and after a few years, we closed it down.

But other than those two instances, we stuck closely to what we knew and continued to enjoy great success. Frankly, I would have continued on, but we decided to sell because none of the kids wanted to run it—and they all had worked at the business at one time or another. Arnold, who had had several bouts with cancer, was exhausted and wanted to retire. Harvey was, as he put it, "tired of mopping the floors" (we had about twelve hundred employees at the time, so Harvey never touched a mop, at least, not at the business) and I didn't want to be responsible for the family wealth by myself.

Staples had been after us for several years to sell to them. So I called Tom Stemberg and told him we were willing to sell. We met with him and his team several times and came to terms. But then I had seller's remorse and backed out. In the meantime, Staples' stock price increased. I called Tom again and told him that now that they could afford to pay more, we would go forward with the deal. He agreed, but only if I assured him that this time we would complete the deal.

I told him that we would, but only on three conditions. First, that they would keep Quill as a separate entity, keeping our Quill-branded products and our Quill mailings. Second, they would keep all our people except in the case of poor performance. Third, they would give our people equal pay and benefits to what they were already receiving. Tom Stemberg and Ron Sargent, who succeeded Tom as Chairman, agreed to this, and the deal was done.

In other words, they would keep Quill running pretty much as we had run it. It's often the case that a company that buys another successful company begins to change it, shedding employees and eventually destroying what they bought. We did not want that to happen to Quill, so we did not shop the deal at all. We knew Staples, we were happy with the price, and we knew they would keep their word. They did. Today Quill remains a strong force in the industry. They have subsequently told me it was the best acquisition they had ever made. Everything was exactly as we said it would be and now, eighteen years later, as they have told me, they have been afraid to touch anything about the operation, because it keeps grinding out profits for them. In the meantime, our major mail-order competitor, who sold to the highest bidder, has disappeared, absorbed into that bidder's business, losing much of its value.

The way the deal was structured, we had to sell them all the real estate, the nine distribution centers and the headquarters building, but not the extra land around it. They didn't want the buildings, and we didn't want to sell them, but legally we couldn't do the deal as it was structured without selling them the real estate. So we sold it and we got a more than fair price for it. Another part of the deal was that it had to be done for stock, not cash. Knowing what I now know about the stock market, I would never do that again. But, as luck would have it, it worked out well for us. Howard, who negotiated the deal for us, worked it so we could sell half the stock within a few months and the other half within a year after that. Before the first sale, the stock went up nicely. And before we sold the rest a year later, it had another nice increase. Except for the fact that we knew Staples and the industry so well, selling for stock could have been a disaster.

I agreed to stay on for a year and a half after the sale. Harvey and Arnold wanted to retire immediately. Tom wanted me to have a work contract, but I didn't want one. "Tom," I told him, "If I piss you off, you fire me and if you piss me off, I will quit." I stayed for the full term.

Before we sold the business, on the business front, things were going well. But on the personal side, disaster struck again. In 1992, Audrey was diagnosed with an incurable form of lung cancer. She was given just six months to live. We consulted every doctor we could find but the diagnosis always came back the same. She began getting chemo treatments and we continued living our lives as best as we could, in as normal a fashion as we could.

When the girls were old enough to take care of themselves, Aud had started working at the company in the advertising department, but after starting the treatments, it wasn't long before she was unable to keep working. She lived for two more years instead of six months, passing away on July 15, 1994. As I am writing this, twenty-three years later, I am still tearing up. Shortly before she died, as she was lying on the sofa one evening, exhausted and much thinner than she'd been when she was healthy, I said to her, "I wish I could have given you much more." Her reply was, "Jack, you gave me everything I had always wanted, security." I believe she meant financial security and, I like to believe, even more, the security of a strong and loving relationship of forty years.

By giving me the room to work fifty- and sixty-hour weeks and more, never complaining and never demanding more than we could afford, she was a true partner in our success. A balanced life? Not by today's definition. Yes, I worked at the business, and she worked taking care of the children and the house. I really focused on the business to the exclusion of much else. I know that's out of fashion now, but it worked for us. Aud loved her part in the partnership and she was great at it. She loved to cook and to sew and to take care of the house and the kids.

And when she started working again, she enjoyed that too—enjoyed her relationships with others in her department, never having lunch with me, but with them. She was a quiet, but strong person, someone everyone loved. People would talk with her, and then walk away thinking it was a great conversation, not realizing that she had done almost none of the talking and most of the listening. Aud attended all the industry events with me and acted as my phone contact list. She remembered everyone's name, how many kids they had, etc., and often, as we met them at events, she filled me in as they approached, so I wouldn't be embarrassed.

For the next six years after she passed away, I tried dating at my daughters' insistence. Without Aud there to act as my memory bank, I used my computer. Every time I called someone—and everyone was giving me names to call—I would enter their details on the computer so I would remember what they had told me. I would review the entries before I dated them and then add to the entries after I dated them. Eventually, I had thirty-six dossiers on the computer before I met Goldie, who had been a major success in commercial real estate in Chicago and who had just sold her company, and that ended my dating. It also opened up a new and very interesting chapter in my life.

Right before we sold the company, my daughter, Judith, suggested we start a family office because she was tired of paying bills herself. With the sale coming up and with the need to handle all that money, we thought it was a good idea. So we hired someone to head up the family office and now, almost twenty years later, he is still with us and the family office has grown into another enterprise involving everyone in Harvey's family and mine, plus a full staff. It has become a very complete and very successful endeavor.

Our family office has grown to be a family business in itself. Through it we handle all of our investments, pay our taxes, handle our philanthropic endeavors, and plan for the future. Harvey and I have stepped down as co-chairmen and one of his sons, Steve, and one of my daughters, Sheri, are now co-chairs. As part of preparing for the future, the third generation (G3), our grandchildren, are now involved with the investing and the philanthropy, and several are working in our real estate company. Our goal is typically American, not just preserving wealth but also growing it and being productive, contributing citizens. And one of the best and most satisfying endeavors, for me, is preserving and passing on the principles that served us well, principles that I believe have made America so great.

One thing we did when we sold the company was to start developing some of the land around our corporate headquarters, so that by the time the sale was complete, we moved into office space in a new office building we had built. From there, as the family office expanded, we moved into bigger space in a second office building we built across the street from the first. I can still see the Quill headquarters from my office in that building.

The only regret I had after selling Quill was not realizing the power we had in our organization and in the profits we were generating and accumulating. We had grown to over $630 million in sales with about twelve hundred employees nationwide. With over eight hundred thousand customers, and with all that strength, we could have expanded into other product categories, such as shipping-room supplies and more. We could have grown the business even more, much more. But we were too busy running the business when we had perfectly capable managers and VPs who could have run it themselves, and did after we sold, while we explored more opportunities.

On the other hand, there were some memorable events in those years that still give me great pleasure. The first is that after I was the second honoree for an industry City of Hope dinner (we raised about $135,000), I started a council for The City of Hope, a very large cancer research center and hospital in Duarte, California. I ran it for about twenty years or so until we sold. At the last dinner I attended (2017), they gave The City of Hope a check for $14.8 million. Overall, since we began this initiative, the industry has raised $175 million for them.

The second is a U.S. Supreme Court case that we (Quill) won in 1992, *Quill Corp. v. North Dakota* (504 U.S. 298 (1992)). It's a case that is often mentioned in the press. North Dakota sued us to try to make us collect sales tax for sales we made in their state. We refused, saying we had no nexus (presence) in their state. We won in their Lower Court, and they appealed to the State Supreme Court, where they won. We appealed to the U.S. Supreme Court and we won. And that is why, to this day, most people do not pay any tax on what they buy through the internet or mail order. Every time I read about this in the papers, I imagine our older brother, Arnold, who led the charge on this, dancing in his grave. But just this year, 2018, the Supreme Court has overturned that decision. Sad.

And so ends forty-three years of a great, fulfilling adventure. And a new chapter begins.

17

AN ENTREPRENEUR'S PATH TO PHILANTHROPY

Philanthropy had not been a part of my upbringing. Dad never made a lot of money, so there wasn't that much to give away. But, for me, philanthropy started in the 1960s, when there was an appeal for money to support Israel during one of its wars. I was barely making a living then, but I gave a thousand dollars, and that was the start of my philanthropic efforts. As we began making more money, Audrey and I began giving more to our Temple and to other organizations.

For many years, Aud, the girls, and I sat around the table at the beginning of each December and went through all the requests we had received during the year, and just picked out those we all agreed to give to. Also, at the company, we set aside a certain percentage of the profit each year and my brothers and I would decide what to donate to. Then, after we sold the company, and Israel was in another of its wars, there was another call for financial support. My brothers and I decided that we would each give a million dollars—a long road from that first thousand.

After the sale of the business, we each set up our own foundations and pursued our own interests. I hired someone to run my foundation and handle all the paperwork, but after a few years, I found I had made a mistake in the person I had hired. She wasn't doing much research on who we were going to give to, didn't write good agreements, and didn't follow up to make sure our money was used as intended. However, I didn't discover that until after I had invested eight million dollars in a failed effort.

I have peripheral neuropathy, a very painful and debilitating nerve condition. I got it right after Audrey died, and Goldie blames it on my emotional distress. The doctors have no idea what caused it. They call it idiopathic, which means they have no clue as to what caused it, or how to cure it.

Seven or eight years after I was diagnosed with it, and after I remarried, Goldie and I attended a support group meeting where people exchanged information on what treatment or drugs they were using. All the stories were sad. After a while, I spoke up and said, "No one is talking about finding a cure." Someone else said, "That would cost a lot. If you are a millionaire, maybe you could do that." I thought to myself, I am a millionaire and I will. That was the beginning of a journey that led down one very expensive blind alley and then to many more expensive years of further efforts.

But that blind alley experience taught me a very important lesson in philanthropy. Serious philanthropy is a business. You are investing significant money and you should expect results. And, most importantly, donor's intent should be sacrosanct.

That eight million dollars had been pledged to a topflight medical research hospital to fund a chair for a research scientist and to equip laboratories to search for a cure for peripheral neuropathy. The scientist was hired, and the laboratories equipped, and most of the money had been spent—when someone else came along with a grant to study some other nerve condition, which they then pursued. When I threatened to sue, they returned the unspent money, as called for in the contract. But that was just one million out of the eight. A very expensive lesson learned.

Since then I have met and heard of hundreds of similar cases: it seems as if many institutions will promise to do whatever a donor wants and is willing to support, and then, once they get the money, they spend part or all of it on something different. It seems to me that if they don't want to do what a donor wants to contribute for, they shouldn't accept the money. That is the only ethical thing to do.

I fired the person running my foundation and began interviewing for a new director. Alicia, Goldie's daughter, who is a lawyer, was visiting us in Florida with her children and husband while I was interviewing a candidate at our home there. She sat in on the interview and after the candidate left, she said, "I would like that job. I can't take the long hours my job requires and also raise my kids, and I can do your job." So I hired her, and our philanthropic efforts have since become very professional and businesslike, with a staff of three, a board of directors (which some of the grandchildren now sit on), and tight contracts with all our major giving recipients.

We have become very focused in our giving, dividing up our dollars into major categories, including freedom, Jewish, medical, and other, meaning civic causes, etc. We look at our giving as investing. In most cases, we invest in organizations that are doing things we think are important, whether it's the local theater or a children's hospital, but we don't put in much of our time.

In other cases, we either get more involved or, where we don't find an organization doing what we want to get done, we start our own organization. For Goldie, who was a topflight commercial real estate broker in Chicago, it is "The Goldie B. Wolfe Miller Women Leaders in Real Estate Initiative," now referred to as "The Goldie Initiative." It provides scholarships for women in real estate to get their master's degrees. She also has developed networking events, job fairs, and other efforts. It is becoming quite successful, having spread from one university in Chicago to nine, including one in Wisconsin. She spends a good deal of time on it and gets a lot of pleasure from it.

For my daughter Judith, the cause is alternative medicine. She has attended innumerable conferences all across the country and has become a practitioner in the field, working with clients in person or on the phone. She has also written a book, *How to Survive Your Teenager*, and has appeared on a number of radio and TV programs. She is currently working on a new book.

My daughter Sheri started her own center, the Charmm'd Foundation "for Strengthening You and Your Organization through Peer Advisory Groups, Training and Workshops and Executive Coaching." Her focus, according to her website, is "providing leadership development to strengthen leaders of tax-exempt organizations" in various communities along the North Shore of the Chicago area. She has three very dedicated and competent people working with her. Sheri has taken many courses and has become a certified coach in this area. She puts in more than full time at this, while still finding time to bond with her two adult children, who are pursuing their own interests. Because of my own slant on things, I keep telling her that she could turn the Charmm'd Foundation into a regular, profit-making business. I think it would be quite successful.

For Bethany, one of my granddaughters, it's the Slingshot Fund, an organization that teaches young adults how to research and select the worthiest Jewish causes to support. Slingshot is a really neat way for the younger generation to learn about thoughtful philanthropy. She has been active in it for the past few years and is now on its board of directors. That keeps her pretty busy, in addition to assuming the role of space designer (which was part of her college major) for her husband, Garett, in his newly established commercial real estate business in Philadelphia, and taking care of their two small children.

My daughters and I started another foundation, the Grandy Foundation, in honor of my late wife. After over a year of discussions, we finally focused on two causes that we felt Aud would have really liked. The first is helping abused women escape their abusive environment and become independent. We were successful in finding an organization called Shalva, which is doing an admirable job in this area, so we simply support them in their work and get reports on the progress of the women we help with our donations. The second area involved more work because there were so few organizations doing what we wanted to do, which was to help young, high-functioning autistic people find meaningful work. These people have much to offer employers because of their unique abilities, but often can't find good jobs because of their poor social skills. Fortunately we found an organization working in the field of autism that has a nonprofit company that employs only high-functioning autistic young adults to do IT-related work.

Alicia, my daughter through my marriage to Goldie, also started her own entrepreneurial philanthropic endeavor. As a result of all the work she has been doing these past ten years with non-profits, she has come to the conclusion that they need help—a lot of help—in training board members to be more effective. So, she has started a program in conjunction with Northwestern University, the Board Member Institute for Jewish Nonprofits, to train them in all the responsibilities expected of a board member.

As for me, the category I give the most attention (and money) to is the freedom category. I define the freedom category as anything that supports individual freedom as expressed in our Declaration of Independence. My main focus is education. And within the freedom category, the place I put most of the money is in the Jack Miller Center, as discussed earlier.

18

KEEPING BUSY
AND HAPPY
TOWARD THE END

So here I am, at the age of eighty-nine and looking forward to several more years of active life, if I keep all my marbles. I belong to two country clubs, one near our main residence in Bannockburn, near Chicago, and one near my winter home in Palm Beach Gardens, Florida. However, I can't play golf anymore because I have an inoperable back problem. But that doesn't bother me because I never became very good, just shooting in the nineties. I didn't start playing until I was in my late sixties. While building the business, there just wasn't time for it. On the other hand, Goldie plays a lot, having started after we got married. And I don't play, and am not interested in playing, bridge.

So what does the future look like? Well, very importantly, to me, I continue to work out every day, alternating swimming laps with time on the Lifecycle, weights, and stretching in the gym. That's been a lifelong practice since the age of thirteen. I also have two other major projects.

The first is building the real estate business, Millbrook. As I have already mentioned, we began by building out an office and industrial park on land we had acquired around our Quill headquarters. Then we went outside that area and bought a small office building. Soon after that, the 2008 crash came, and we were approached to buy another office building park of four good-sized buildings at fire-sale prices. We were able to do that as a buyer with available cash who could close the deal quickly. The buildings were from about 60 percent leased to near-zero percent and needed some repairs. We fixed them up, leased them, and they have become a well-performing asset. So we were on the way to getting into the real estate business in a much bigger way.

Since then we have acquired more buildings in the Chicago suburban market, and one in Milwaukee, and several more in Philadelphia. One of my granddaughters married a young engineer who saw what we were doing in Chicago and wanted to get into real estate in Philadelphia. He found a good deal on a modestly sized office building there, so I bought the building. And, with a lot of help from our Millbrook people in Buffalo Grove, the Chicago area location, he began to learn the real estate business by working at it and handling all parts of it. A good but rough way to learn.

In any event, my vision is that Millbrook is the new family business. I am fortunate to have two grandchildren in the third generation who want to build it. I am very much involved, and given a few more years, they will be well along in experience. We now have a decent-sized (and growing) portfolio of buildings, plus a terrific management team and great staff of over seventy building managers and engineers. Also, with her terrific experience in the field, Goldie has been, and will be, a great resource. So that is one thing that is keeping me very engaged.

The second major project is the Jack Miller Center for Teaching America's Founding Principles and History (JMC). Of all the things I have ever done with my philanthropic dollars, this is the one effort that has given me the most pleasure and yielded the best results. We started a few years earlier, but then incorporated in 2007 as an independent non-profit with headquarters in Philadelphia. When we began, we had one hundred twenty-five political science and history professors in our network who shared our mission. Today, we have nine hundred professors in our network on three hundred college campuses. Phenomenal growth! In 2016, we launched an initiative in Chicago at the high school level to help teachers improve civic education in their schools.

There is hardly a day that goes by that you don't see an article in *The Wall Street Journal* about problems in our education system. One of the problems often mentioned is that American history and the founding principles, or civic literacy, is seldom taught. Our goal at the Miller Center is to reintroduce that teaching into the schools.

Our strength is our community of professors across the country, the constant growth of that community, and the enthusiasm we keep generating through them. Very importantly, the effort will also be made possible as donors who are interested in education increasingly see that we can be the best stewards of their philanthropic dollars. If they are interested in this area of education at any level, we can make sure their philanthropic dollars will have the greatest impact.

So, all in all, life is still interesting. Like most people my age, I have physical problems. Peripheral neuropathy and a bad back are chief among them. A pacemaker and four stents are also a part of that mix. But life remains good and the challenges are invigorating.

I have had a good life. My late wife, Audrey, was a perfect partner as I was building the business, working very long hours. My wife, my family, and my in-laws couldn't have been better. When Audrey died it was a tough blow. And then the next six years of being single was not a great period. I dated a lot of women, about thirty-six of them, according to the computerized records I kept in order to remember names and other information. But then Goldie came along and changed all of that: she still jokes about my computerized records and complains that because her last name was Wolfe, the computer listed her last.

After dating for a while, she decided we were going to get more serious. That ended my dating of other women; we were soon married and have now been happily married for eighteen years. Goldie has opened up a whole different life for me. While Audrey was a strong but quiet person who was happy to cook and bake and focus on the domestic side of life, Goldie had spent her life as a single mom who became very successful as a commercial real estate broker, and then with her own business.

Without the time demands of an operating business and with Goldie, my life went into a whole different phase. Goldie, in many ways, is the opposite of Audrey. Audrey was very comfortable living a quiet life that revolved around the home. Goldie, on the other hand, was a successful businessperson, used to being a much more public figure. She had a much wider circle of friends and acquaintances and enjoyed all those interactions. So, suddenly, my social life exploded.

Also, since Goldie is seventeen years younger than me, her daughter was just graduating from college, so I was there when she graduated law school, got married and had children. (I even introduced Alicia to Aaron, whom she married.) And because Goldie is a traditional doting grandmother and I had the time, I was able to be much more a part of Alicia's children's lives at that age than I had been with my other grandchildren's lives.

Goldie also became an active participant in everything I was involved with, serving with me on the board of the Miller Center, the family foundation, the Peripheral Neuropathy Board, the board of the investment committee, Millbrook Properties, the real estate company where her experience is a great asset, and more.

She has made a major effort to reach out to my daughters and grandchildren while I have become very involved with Alicia and her family so there is a great relationship all the way around. So I not only married Goldie, but I expanded my family. And, somehow, two successful CEOs are managing to happily live together.

Our daughters are still pursuing their own passions and, although they have faced some challenges, they have remained strong and seem to be enjoying their lives. And my grandchildren are all getting off to a good start in their lives. My ties with my business and life partner, my brother Harvey, are as strong as ever and we still work together in real estate and in other areas where our interests are aligned. Arnold, unfortunately, died several years ago, succumbing to the cancer that had been the original impetus to selling the business. One other project I am working on is to help all of my children and grandchildren in their careers, passing on what I have learned and the work ethic and culture that helped me in my life.

Howard and I are still great friends, having at least one conversation a week to solve the world's problems, and we see each other often. He is very proud of the fact that five of his grandchildren are CPAs, while I am proud of all the entrepreneurial efforts in my own family.

So, all in all, life has been good and I am enthusiastically looking forward to the remaining years ahead, to building the real estate business and the Miller Center. I have ambitious plans for both. My greatest fear is that, while life is so good, we may forget what made it so and thus undermine what we have done. I am leaving my grandchildren some inheritance, a history of my ethics and views on life, which I hope will help guide them in their lives. But most of all, I hope to leave them an America still founded on the principles of freedom—personal, individual freedom, one in which they can prosper and contribute, through their own efforts.

Finally, while writing this short book about why I started the Miller Center and what I have dreamed about accomplishing, I kept thinking about a play I saw when I was just sixteen years old or so. On one of the first real dates I had in high school, in the days when the love of country was so strong, my date and I went downtown to see the musical *Brigadoon*, which is about a Scottish town that appears for just one day every hundred years. So I googled it just to remind myself what it was about.

Two American tourists, Tommy and Jeff, lose their way in the Scottish Highlands. They hear music and follow its sound to a fair in a town not shown on their map. Tommy falls madly in love with Fiona, a young maiden from the town. The Americans learn that the town appears only for a single day every hundred years to protect it from being changed by the outside world. An outsider can stay in the town only if he or she loves someone in the town enough to "give up everything and stay with that one person." Tommy isn't sure that he loves Fiona enough to give up everything.

So, as the day ends, the town disappears, and Tommy and Jeff go back to New York. But Tommy can't forget Fiona, and he and Jeff return to Scotland, to the spot where the town appeared. Magically, the town reappears. The schoolmaster of the town, Mr. Lundie, explains, "Tommy, lad! . . . Ye mus' really love her. You woke me up." When Tommy stares at him in astonishment, Mr. Lundie replies, "You shouldna be too surprised, lad. I told ye when ye love someone deeply, anythin' is possible. Even miracles" (Richards 1973). Then Tommy waves goodbye to Jeff and disappears with Mr. Lundie into the Highland mist to be reunited with Fiona.

Before he returned to Scotland to find Fiona again, when he was daydreaming about his lost true love, Tommy had lamented, "Why do people have to lose things to find out what they really mean?"

I hope and pray that we don't become like Brigadoon, disappearing into the mist until someone once again discovers the wonderful truths that have made America so great. We shouldn't have to lose what is so good about our country and lament, like Tommy, "Why do people have to lose things to find out what they really mean?"

I hope and pray that we and our children and our children's children learn the principles of freedom that have made America so great, and that our love for America and its principles remains so strong, that it never disappears into the mist until some people, a hundred years or so later, once again rediscover that love of freedom.

My mother Ida's family. I'm seated in the first row on the left. *Source: Jack Miller Family*

My high school yearbook picture—1947. *Source: Jack Miller Family*

A weight-lifting contest—my freshman year at the University of Illinois-Champagne—1947. *Source: Jack Miller Family*

The hand-balancing act my friend Howard Bernstein and I had in college. *Source: Jack Miller Family*

I'm the bottom man. *Source: Jack Miller Family*

We played county fairs and clubs. *Source: Jack Miller Family*

Me at 19 years of age. *Source: Jack Miller Family*

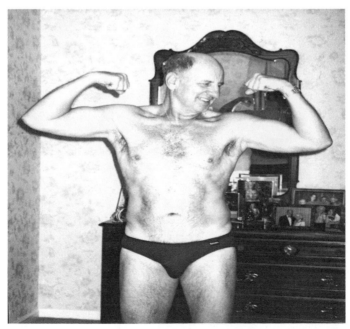

Here I am at 70 years—a bit different, less hair, but not too bad—a testament to consistent workouts. I'm looking forward to the same pose when I reach 90. *Source: Jack Miller Family*

As a traveling salesman in front of City Hall—St. Paul, Minnesota, 1954. *Source: Jack Miller Family*

Audrey and I on our wedding day—October 25, 1954. *Source: Jack Miller Family*

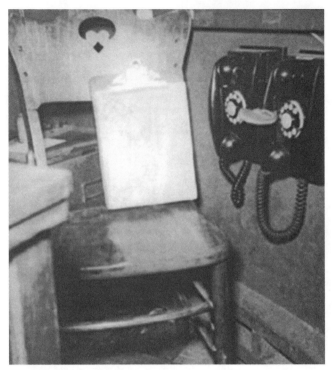

I'm a one-man operation with a phone in Dad's chicken store.
Source: Jack Miller Family

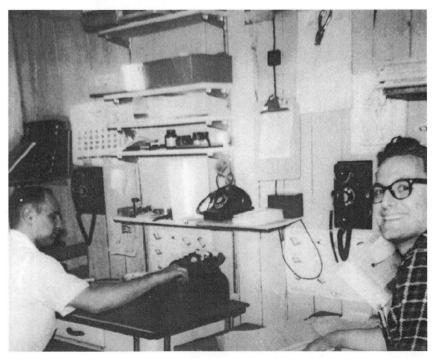

Harvey and I in our office in the converted coal bin office—1957. *Source: Jack Miller Family*

We purchased the 27,000 sq. ft. building on Belmont
Avenue in Chicago as a new headquarters in 1965—
Our first entry into the commercial real estate business.
Source: Jack Miller Family

Our headquarters in Lincolnshire, Illinois (plus 8 distribution centers open around the country). In
between, a journey of 23 years of hard work. *Source: Jack Miller Family*

My grandson and I raising the flag on the newly installed flagpole in front of the Quill headquarters in Lincolnshire in 1980, perhaps foreshadowing my interest in learning about the teaching of our founding principles and history. *Source: Jack Miller Family*

Ve care" about being the best supplier you have ever had!

Officers of Quill Corporation (from left to right):   Jack, Arnie, Harvey.

IR PROMISES TO YOU...

receive quality products priced to save you money.

products we sell are among the finest on the market today. We offer us national brands, as well as our own Quill brand supplies. And rdless of the quantity you buy, our everyday discounts prices are below those in most other office supply catalogs.

r order is usually shipped within 48 hours.

large, modern warehouse allows us to keep almost everything in

WE GUARANTEE YOUR COMPLETE SATISFACTION 2 WAYS:

1. WE GUARANTEE OUR PRODUCTS—You must be completely satisfied with every item you purchase at Quill. It must be as we describe it and just what you expect it to be.

2. WE GUARANTEE OUR SERVICE—You must be satisfied with the way your order is handled and the promptness of shipping. You have every right to expect the best!

If you are displeased with either the product ordered or the service

A page from the Quill catalog showing the Miller brothers in their sophisticated computer room and the irrevocable pledge to give their customers fanatical customer service. *Source: Jack Miller Family*

With Harvey (L) and Arnold (R) in the warehouse of our Lincolnshire facility. *Source: Jack Miller Family*

Goldie and I on our wedding day—February 12, 2000. *Source: Jack Miller Family*

During my career I received many awards, including this from the American-Israel Chamber of Commerce. *Source: Jack Miller Family*

The Chicago Business Leaders (Hall of Fame); The City of Hope (Spirit of Life). *Source: Jack Miller Family*

Distinguished Service—Board of Directors—Direct Marketing
Association, 1985–1991. *Source: Jack Miller Family*

Northwood University (Outstanding Business Leader). *Source: Jack Miller Family*

EPILOGUE

Michael L. Andrews

Jack Miller's love for his country and his gratitude for the liberty that made his own success possible are an inspiration to the staff of the Jack Miller Center and to our network of educators throughout the United States. As president of the Jack Miller Center, it is my honor to lead an organization with a mission so important to our nation's future and to the flourishing of its people.

I think it is important that as an organization we never lose sight of the purpose that drives our work day to day. Jack founded our Center because he believes in the importance of educating future generations in the principles the United States was founded upon. He recognized that students were not learning about America's heritage and our unique form of government, so he offered a vision for a Center that would ensure that the study and teaching of the principles underlying free societies would be renewed and thrive on college campuses across the country.

But why is this so important? Why focus on the origins of the American Founding?

Free societies are rare in human history. If one were to employ Aristotle's typology for categorizing regimes according to whether power is vested in the one, the few, or the many, one could comfortably assert that rule by the one or the few have been the predominant form for the majority of recorded history. Not only are societies founded on the consent of the governed rare, but it is often said that they are fragile. Their rarity and brevity have always seemed linked. As James Madison put it in *Federalist* 10 when speaking of ancient democracies, free societies were "as short in their lives as they have been violent in their deaths" (Rossiter 2003, 76). Indeed, their fragility is often involved as one of the chief arguments for studying the foundations of free societies in order to keep their freedoms secure.

But what are the sources of this fragility? The fact that free societies are rare, often unstable, and that even those few with demonstrated longevity (such as the Roman Republic) nevertheless collapsed, should command our attention just as it did the Founders'. Among other things, the Founders studied the dissolution of the Roman Republic not out of antiquarian curiosity, but because of their keen, very real-world concern that their own fledgling experiment could meet the same ignominious fate. After all, didn't the historical record show that such experiments almost always fail; did it not show the dangerous impracticality of governments based in some form of popular sovereignty—that they are inherently unstable and prone to degenerating into mob rule and eventual tyranny; did it not ultimately show the folly of entrusting ordinary people with self-government, given that history seemed to demonstrate that the people couldn't exercise power well, much less rule their own turbulent passions?

The question of fragility is always worth raising, and not simply because one could cite contemporary examples of regimes which seemed, for a season, to be steadily moving toward liberal democracy—only to reverse course, in some cases with what seems to be the broad support of their own people. The question remains pressing because the fragility of free societies is something that is said to inhere in their very nature. Hence the importance of understanding their strengths and weaknesses. Hence the necessity of an education in the foundations of free societies—not simply for one's edification, nor solely to be a better-informed citizen, but perhaps most importantly to help ensure their perpetuation.

The answer to the fragility question lies in part with a certain tension in human nature—a tension that the Founders reflected upon in their own ruminations on the subject. One sees the tension by comparing the claims about human nature in the Declaration of Independence to some of the more somber warnings about human nature found in *The Federalist Papers* and other writings.

The Declaration of Independence laid the foundation for a society based not on ethnicity, race, blood, tribal loyalty, class, rank, or hierarchy, but on the principle "that all Men are created equal, that they are endowed by their Creator with certain unalienable Rights, that among these are Life, Liberty, and the Pursuit of Happiness." Along with the successful prosecution of the Revolution and the establishment of the Constitution, the Declaration is rightly acknowledged as one of the Founding's great and historic achievements.

The political order the Founders created was based on the belief that human beings were not so different that one could ever legitimately assert the right to rule another *by nature*. At the same time, however, and as Madison's admonition that "men are not angels" reminds us, the Founders worried ceaselessly about the human inclination to dominate others—an inclination from which their own countrymen were not immune. As Jack points out, this explains in large part their desire to limit the powers of government, to divide political authority through such institutional arrangements as the separation of powers and federalism, and to guarantee individual rights. The political order they founded did indeed rest on the belief that human beings were by nature free and equal, but they also knew that while individuals might insist on their own rights being respected, they might not always be so charitable with the rights of others. As Jefferson said in his First Inaugural, "the minority possess their equal rights, which equal law must protect, and to violate would be oppression" (Jefferson 1987, 141). But as the bitter partisan struggles between the Federalists and the Jeffersonian Republicans attest, honoring the equal rights of others, particularly in the case of the Alien and Sedition Acts, was at times easier in principle than in practice. And, one has to add, nowhere was the contradiction between principle and practice more glaring, and tragic, than in the institution of slavery.

The fact that the Founders were successful in laying the foundation for a political culture where the respect for the equal rights of others, and not simply one's own rights, eventually became the norm (after titanic struggles), is a monumental achievement, and one we perhaps take for granted. But it remains a fragile one, as contemporary debates over free speech, among other things, show. On college campuses it has become increasingly common for certain groups to demand that their voices be heard, to the exclusion or suppression of others. Nor is this problem peculiar to America. It seems, rather, a perennial difficulty in establishing and maintaining free societies. One need only briefly glance at recent efforts to establish free societies in the Middle East. Most Iraqis welcomed their liberation from Saddam Hussein's dictatorial rule. Sadly, they seemed much less willing to respect their neighbor's right to be equally free in his person and property.

The Founders created a political order that explicitly eschewed a tribal, ethnic, or religious foundation. But they were under no illusions that tribal loyalties, sectarian passions, or, in short, the human tendency to form factions would vanish. They hoped to moderate them, but they knew that as long as people are free, and free to form attachments to party or sect, factions would always exist. As Madison observed in *Federalist* 10:

> "Liberty is to faction what air is to fire, an aliment without which it instantly expires. But it could not be a less folly to abolish liberty, which is essential to political life, because it nourishes faction than it would be to wish the annihilation

of air, which is essential to animal life, because it imparts to fire its destructive agency" (Rossiter 2003, 73).

The Founders were right to believe that ordinary human beings are indeed capable of self-government while honoring the equal rights of others. At the same time, there were powerful forces at work in human nature that had to be overcome to establish a stable and flourishing free society. As the educator E. D. Hirsch noted:

> The history of tribal and racial hatreds is the history and prehistory of human-kind. . . . Our brilliant political tradition cannot altogether remove the instinct of tribalism, with its innate dislike and suspicion of the other, but it is the best system yet devised for counteracting it. . . . This vast, artificial, transtribal construct is what our Founders aimed to achieve. And they understood that it can be achieved effectively only by intelligent schooling. (Hirsch 2009, 86)

So, intelligent schooling should always include a close reading of the writings of the Founders themselves and the thinkers who influenced them. This includes the great works of the Western tradition. The goal is not simply to help the young become more educated citizens, nor simply to instill a deeper appreciation of the fragility of free societies and the immense, centuries-long effort it took to establish them, though these are always laudable, and arguably, essential goals in and of themselves. Through patient study of the great works of the West, one hopes, students will also come to a better understanding of their own all too human nature. It is this self-knowledge that one hopes will lead them not only to cherish their own liberty, but to cherish the inalienable right of others to the same blessing.

WORKS CITED

Amar, Akhil. 2016. "Constitution Day: Miami University 2016." Filmed September 22, 2016, at the Janus Forum Constitution Day Program, Miami University, Oxford, OH. Video, 1:12:28. Accessed April 23, 2018. https://www.jackmillercenter.org/constitution-day/constitution-day-events/.

Hirsch, E. D., Jr. 2009. *The Making of Americans*. New Haven: Yale University Press.

Jefferson, Thomas. 1987. "First Inaugural Address." In *The Founders' Constitution* Vol. 1, Ch. 4.33. Edited by Philip B. Kurland and Ralph Lerner. Chicago: University of Chicago Press.

———. 1826. Thomas Jefferson to Roger C. Weightman, June 24, 1826. Accessed April 23, 2018. https://www.loc.gov/exhibits/jefferson/214.html.

Lazarus, Emma. 1883. "The New Colossus." Accessed April 23, 2018. https://www.poets.org/poetsorg/poem/new-colossus.

Lee, Simon. 2015. "Lord Denning, Magna Carta and Magnanimity." *Denning Law Journal* 27:106–129.

Locke, John. 1988. *Two Treatises of Government*. Edited by Peter Laslett. Cambridge: Cambridge University Press.

McDougall, Walter A. 2004. *Freedom Just around the Corner*. New York: Harper Collins.

Miller, Jack. 2008. *Simply Success: How to Start, Build, and Grow a Multimillion-Dollar Business—the Old-Fashioned Way*. Hoboken, NJ: John Wiley & Sons.

Reagan, Ronald. 1961. "Encroaching Control." Speech to the Phoenix Chamber of Commerce, March 30, 1961. Transcript and MP3 audio, 43:29. Accessed April 23, 2018. https://archive.org/details/RonaldReagan-EncroachingControl.

Richards, Stanley, ed. 1973. *Ten Great Musicals of the American Theatre*. With an introduction and notes on the plays, authors, and composers. Radnor, PA: Chilton Book Company.

Rossiter, Clinton, ed. 2003. *The Federalist Papers*. With an introduction and notes by Charles R. Kesler. New York: Signet Classics.

Sacks, Jonathan, trans. 2015. *Pirkei Avot*. Jerusalem: Koren Publishers.

Tocqueville, Alexis de. 2000. *Democracy in America*. Translated and edited by Harvey Mansfield and Delba Winthrop. Chicago: University of Chicago Press.

U.S. Department of Education. 2010. "Overview: What is the U.S. Department of Education?" Accessed April 23, 2018. https://www2.ed.gov/about/overview/focus/what.html.

RESOURCES

SUMMARY OF PROGRAMS, FELLOWSHIPS, AND INITIATIVES

The mission of the Jack Miller Center for Teaching America's Founding Principles and History is to reinvigorate education in America's founding principles and history—an education vital to thoughtful and engaged citizenship.

As a non-profit public charity, the Center is supported by a growing community of donors who believe it is essential to ensure that our young citizens understand the principles and institutions of the nation. Such knowledge is central to preserving our freedoms for future generations.

The organization works to advance the teaching and study of America's history, its political and economic institutions, and the central principles, ideas and issues arising from the American and Western traditions—all of which continue to animate our national life.

How the JMC Achieves its Goals

- Identifies and invests in professors and teachers who will develop and deliver this curriculum directly to students
- Conducts national programs to support the work and careers of JMC faculty partners
- Supports campus centers that expand the curriculum and engage students
- Connects JMC faculty with other scholars to collaborate and expand their impact

Progress in Higher Education

- Grown from 159 JMC fellows in 2007 to 900 scholars on more than 300 campuses
- More than 800,000 students have taken courses taught by JMC fellows since 2007
- More than 20,000 courses in American ideas and institutions have been taught by JMC fellows
- Awarded 171 postdoctoral fellowships
- Developed 60 centers of research and teaching on campuses around the country

Core Programs

Summer Programs for New Scholars

Intensive Summer Institutes led by eminent historians and political theorists introduce up-and-coming professors into JMC's nationwide faculty community and support their career development.

Postdoctoral Teaching Fellowships

These fellowships support the career advancement of the most promising, dedicated young scholars, creating 21st-century college educators who will shape education on campuses for decades to come.

Lincoln Symposium in American Political Thought

Primarily intended to support scholarship in American political thought among tenure-track professors, this highly reviewed symposium provides scholars the rare opportunity to present their works and receive personal feedback from multiple peers prior to submission for publication to their chosen press.

American Political Thought: A Journal of Ideas, Institutions, and Culture

The first peer-reviewed academic journal focused entirely on American political thought, now subscribed to internationally by more than 6,000 colleges and universities, is co-sponsored by JMC and Notre Dame and is published by the University of Chicago Press.

Constitution Day Initiative

Engaging campus events led by leading scholars and public servants to raise student awareness and interest in the role and meaning of the U.S. Constitution in observance of Constitution Day, September 17. JMC's website also contains a Constitution Day resource center with a growing selection of texts relating to constitutional issues.

High School Teacher Initiatives

Led by JMC university faculty partners, the Civic Education Outreach program provides graduate and professional development programs for high school teachers to improve civic education at the high school level.

Special Projects

Curricular initiatives, special symposia, panels at national professional conferences, and other events and programs offer new avenues to promote research, scholarship, and the teaching of America's founding principles and history.

To learn more, please visit www.jackmillercenter.org.

INDEX

ABOUT THE AUTHOR AND CONTRIBUTORS

Jack Miller is a prominent Chicago area entrepreneur and philanthropist. He is the founder and former president/CEO of Quill Corporation, which grew to be the nation's largest independent direct marketer of office products. He is an active philanthropist who serves as chairman of the Jack Miller Family Foundation, which supports the Jewish community and other community efforts. But his main focus and passion centers on preserving the principles that have made America so great. The major initiative in this effort is the Jack Miller Center for Teaching America's Founding Principles and History, where he is a very active chairman of the board. Established in 2004, the initiative is now the dominant force in returning this education to college campuses and to date they have close to a thousand professors on hundreds of campuses. A high school teachers' academy has also been established for history and civics teachers. Jack hopes this will be his legacy to the country he loves so much. As a graduate of the University of Illinois with a degree in journalism, Mr. Miller is also the author of "Simply Success: How to Start, Build and Grow a Multimillion-Dollar Business the Old-Fashioned Way," published by John Wiley and Sons in 2008.

CONTRIBUTORS

Michael Andrews is president of the Jack Miller Center and has been with the center since its inception. Prior to taking the role of president, he led the Jack Miller Center's academic programs and higher-education initiatives. Originally from Helena, Montana, he received a master's degree in European history and a doctorate in American intellectual history, both from Tulane University. Dr. Andrews formerly served on the faculty of St. John's College, teaching at both the Santa Fe and Annapolis campuses.

James W. Ceaser is the Harry F. Byrd professor of politics and director of the Program on Constitutionalism and Democracy at the University of Virginia, where he has taught since 1976. He has held visiting professorships at Harvard, Oxford, University of Basel, University of Bordeaux, and University of Rennes. Professor Ceaser has worked closely with the Jack Miller Center since its inception, serving on the board of directors and as chair of the Academic Council. A recipient of the 2015 Bradley Prize, he has authored many books, including *Presidential Selection*, *Designing a Polity*, and *Reconstructing America*, and he is a frequent contributor to the popular press.